FINANCE & GROW YOUR NEW BUSINESS:
Get a Grip on the Money

numbers
101 for
SMALL BUSINESS

FINANCE & GROW YOUR NEW BUSINESS:
Get a Grip on the Money

Angie Mohr, CA, CMA

Self-Counsel Press
(a division of)
International Self-Counsel Press Ltd.
USA   Canada

Self-Counsel Press acknowledges the financial support of the Government of Canada through the Book Publishing Industry Development Program (BPIDP) for our publishing activities.

Printed in Canada.

First edition: 2008

Library and Archives Canada Cataloguing in Publication

Mohr, Angie
    Finance and grow your new business / Angie Mohr.

ISBN 978-1-55180-820-8

    1. Small business—Finance. 2. Small business—Growth. 3. Small business—Management. 4. Business planning. I. Title.

HD62.7.M636 2008   658.02'2   C2008-900663-1

Screen shot on page 144 from Quickbooks *by Intuit. Used with permission.*

Self-Counsel Press
(a division of)
International Self-Counsel Press Ltd.

1704 North State Street	1481 Charlotte Road
Bellingham, WA 98225	North Vancouver, BC V7J 1H1
USA	Canada

Contents

Checklists

Diagrams

Tables

Samples

Worksheets

Notice to Readers

Laws are constantly changing. Every effort is made to keep this publication as current as possible. However, the author, the publisher, and the vendor of this book make no representations or warranties regarding the outcome or the use to which the information in this book is put and are not assuming any liability for any claims, losses, or damages arising out of the use of this book. The reader should not rely on the author or the publisher of this book for any professional advice. Please be sure that you have the most recent edition.

Acknowledgments

I would like to thank the following people for their assistance and support during the writing of this book:

Everyone at Self-Counsel Press who has provided guidance and encouragement throughout this project. Without the encouragement and expert guidance of my wonderful publishers, this book would not exist.

Sam Hiyate, Ellen Roseman, Dave Chilton, and Dave Trahair for all their advice and encouragement.

All of my accounting and workshop clients who have helped with the direction of the series.

Friends and family, in particular, my husband, Jeff, and Alex and Erika.

McClurkin Ahier and Company, for all of their support during the writing and touring process.

Hancock Askew and Company, for the opportunity to consult for an amazing group of small business clients.

Thanks also to Matt Osborne, one of the finest musicians/small-business owners/human beings I have had the honor of knowing. I will miss you greatly.

Introduction

Entrepreneurs are people with a dream. They build on their skills and abilities and try to provide a stable income for themselves and their families.

There are as many reasons for starting a business as there are entrepreneurs. For some, it's about the money. For others, it's security and stability that are most important. Many entrepreneurs find satisfaction and fulfillment in building something from nothing and witnessing the quickening; that point where the business takes on a life of its own.

The freedom that comes from running your own business, and your successes and failures, is an irresistible pull for most entrepreneurs. This drive is what fuels them and keeps them going even when money is tight and business is bad. This sets them apart from others and makes them a special breed of individuals.

Entrepreneurs quickly learn that starting your own business is incredibly hard work,

and it requires great commitment with little financial reward in the beginning. This book will help explain how you, as an entrepreneur, can get the money you need to finance your business, and how you can manage it on an ongoing basis.

Part One of this book, "Finance Your Business," will cover questions such as—

- What kind of business should I start?
- Should I buy an existing business or start one from scratch?
- What's a business plan?
- Where will I find money to start up?
- How do I find my external advisers?
- How will I know how I stack up against my competition?
- How do I know when it's time to hire people?
- Should I invest in new equipment?
- Where do I get money to expand?

Part Two of this book, "Grow Your Business," will delve deeper into the ongoing process of running your business. Businesses are like machines, and they need monitoring, maintenance and the occasional rebuild. This section will help you look at critical financial processes that separate successful businesses from failures, and teach you how to apply those processes to your growing business.

numbers
101 for
SMALL BUSINESS

Part
1

FINANCE YOUR BUSINESS

So, What Kind of Business Should You Start?

J ust because you are a hairdresser doesn't mean you should start a salon. In this chapter, we'll examine the pros and cons of different types of businesses.

Introduction

Starting a business can be scary, exciting, and fulfilling, all at the same time. Frequently, small businesses are started by people who have been employees in the same industry. For example, hair stylists often open salons and accountants start accounting firms. You may feel that because the industry you've previously worked in is familiar to you, you would be successful at starting a business in this industry.

It's important to keep in mind, however, that building a business, managing a business, and doing what the business does are three

very different activities requiring different skill sets. You may be interested in doing only one of these three things. For example, you may get great pleasure out of hair styling, but have little patience for managing the day-to-day operations of a business. In this case, you will want to reconsider your decision to start a business. No matter how much joy it gives you to "be your own boss" while doing the thing that you do best, you will come to despise all the other tasks that go along with owning and managing a small business. On the other hand, you may love building the business: designing the office space, putting together the marketing plan, forecasting, and building the customer base. You may, however, be thoroughly bored with the management aspect or with doing what the business does. Entrepreneurs who feel this way tend to build a business, get it up and running, sell it,

3

and start all over again. The thrill for them is in the creation process.

If you plan to build your business, manage it, and be its chief employee, make sure that you have the energy and the skills to do all three of those things. If not, you will have to hire other people in those positions that you do not wish to do yourself, or rethink your business plan entirely.

Once you have assessed your strengths and weaknesses in terms of building, managing, and operating a business, it's time to look at your personal goals.

Why Do You Want to Be an Entrepreneur?

Before you jump with both feet into starting a business, take some time to examine your motivations. What is it that is driving you towards starting and running a business? Many small-business owners cite things such as more money, freedom, and empire building as their motivators.

Money

Owning and running a business has the potential for providing you with a higher level of investment return and remuneration than you would receive working for someone else. The profit potential is definitely there, but high profits are a trade-off for high risks. Starting a small business is a risky proposition and you, as the owner, face the potential for financial loss as well as gain. It's important to keep this in mind as you build your business and make sure that you not only have the ability to survive failure, but also the ability to tolerate risk. We will examine business risk in greater detail in Chapter 9.

When small-business owners talk about money, though, they often don't mean that they want money for money's sake. Money means something slightly different to each person, but in general, it represents financial independence, prosperity, and security. The more time you spend planning your business model before you begin, the more likely you will be building a profitable enterprise that will meet your personal financial goals.

Freedom

Many small-business owners like the freedom that comes with not having a boss and being able to make their own decisions. However, with this freedom comes ultimate responsibility for the business, including responsibility for customer satisfaction, working conditions, supplier shortages, product failure, and the economic well-being of your employees. Look at whether you are the type of person who can handle these responsibilities while simultaneously making considered, but quick, decisions on a daily basis.

Empire building

For many small-business owners, the most important consideration is that they are building something that will outlive them and perhaps provide income and stability to future generations. If this is an important consideration to you, it will be critical to make sure that you are building a business that has value, and that the value can be transferred to others through sale of the business or inheritance. The unfortunate reality is that over 80 percent of small businesses do not survive into the next generation but die with their owners.

What Kind of Business Should I Start?

The three major types of businesses are manufacturing, retail/wholesale, and service. There are pros and cons to running each type of business, as well as financial considerations. Let's have a look at the characteristics of each one.

Manufacturing business

Manufacturing involves purchasing raw materials and adding labor and specialized machinery to create a product to be sold to customers. An example is a furniture manufacturer. This type of business would buy lumber from a sawmill, as well as nails, screws, glue, and varnish from a supplier. It would then have its employees use saws, drills, and other tools to turn the lumber into tables, chairs, and other furniture.

A manufacturing environment usually requires a hefty upfront investment in the equipment that will be used in the manufacturing process. Manufacturers also tend to need more highly skilled workers than, for example, a retail business. For these reasons, it is very difficult to start up a manufacturing business on a small scale and expand as you go along.

One of the main benefits of this type of business is that it can service very large customers with very specialized products. For example, a manufacturer can supply the entire North American auto industry with injection-molded fan vents.

Retail/Wholesale business

Retailing and wholesaling involves the purchase and resale of products. A retailer sells the products to the final consumer while the wholesaler is simply an intermediary, selling the product to another business that will ultimately sell it to the final consumer.

Almost every store that you can think of is a retailer. For example, a bookstore will purchase books from the publisher and display them for sale in the store. An example of a wholesaler is an importer that purchases teapots from Japan and sells them to stores, usually in large quantities.

Operating a retail business generally requires rented or purchased display space and therefore requires incurring the fixed costs of running that space right from the beginning. For example, if you wanted to run a variety store, you would have to rent (or buy) a storefront location where customers can drop in during your open hours. On top of that, you will have to invest in the store's inventory, which is usually the largest cost to a retailer. The inventory can cost upward of $100,000 depending on the size and scope of the store. For these reasons, retail businesses are usually quite capital intensive and need financing from the beginning.

Wholesalers, on the other hand, generally don't have to deal with the headaches of display spaces, but they do have to maintain an inventory in a warehouse. Therefore, a wholesale business needs to incur the fixed costs associated with operating a warehouse as well as the cost of purchasing the inventory, which tends to be in larger quantities than a retailer. This also generally requires financing from the beginning.

Service business

A service business encompasses any type of business where the item purchased is not a tangible good but instead is "something that is done." Some examples of service businesses are law and accounting firms, lawn-care businesses, auto shops, and spas.

Service businesses in general require less equipment than manufacturers do, and practically no inventory. Therefore, these types of businesses are generally easier to start on a small scale and require less start-up capital. In fact, service businesses account for the majority of all small businesses in North America.

Service businesses tend to be smaller and more local than manufacturers or wholesalers, because services are provided by people and are generally not able to be shipped by parcel post. It can be logistically difficult to provide services over a wide geographic area. However, business services such as website design, accounting, and data processing are becoming the exception to this rule with the ever-expanding use of email and the Internet.

Eight Questions to Ask Yourself

Before you make a final decision as to what type of business to open, make sure that your personal goals and business goals are synchronized by asking yourself the following questions.

1. What are my personal financial goals?

If you want to retire a millionaire in ten years time and you are going to open a small shoe-repair shop, you may not be able to meet your goals. Analyze where you want to be in five or ten years. Do you want a larger house? Be able to travel the world? Have your retirement fully funded? You'll save yourself much grief down the road if you make sure that the type of business you start will provide you with the money you need for your intended lifestyle.

2. Will this business allow me to have the freedom I want to pursue other things?

If you start a business that is based around you being there all the time, you may not be able to pursue some of your personal goals or even to spend the time to plan and strategize for your business. Having a business that can be systematized to run without your constant presence will allow you more freedom.

3. Is the product or service easily marketable?

Starting a business that has a product or service that is understandable and needed by a large segment of the population is by far easier than developing a new product or service and having to both familiarize potential customers with it and, at the same time, convince them that they need it.

CASE STUDY

Craig Sesco knew from the time he was six years old that he wanted to run his own business some day. His father had owned and operated an Italian bakery since before Craig was born and Craig learned to be an entrepreneur through many years of working in the bakery, doing everything from kneading dough to running the ovens to ordering from suppliers, and, eventually, bookkeeping and cash flow forecasting.

Now Craig was 27 and he felt it was time to strike out on his own. He knew that his father had started his business by doing something he loved and that he was lucky that his passion coincided with consumer tastes, but Craig wanted to pursue a different model. He wanted to determine his best chance for commercial success and build a successful business around that.

The first process that Craig went through was to determine his personal goals. He had married his long-time love, Marnie, two years ago and they had just bought a small house for themselves and their new baby. Craig knew that he didn't want to work the crazy hours his father still put in everyday: up at 4:30 a.m. to start the stone ovens and never falling into bed before 11:00 p.m., after reconciling the day's receipts, preparing the bank deposit, and planning for the next day's purchases. Craig wanted to balance his work time with family time but still wanted to build and run a financially successful business that he could sell by the time he was 50.

Through his analysis, Craig also determined that he didn't want to run a business with huge start-up costs and large inventory levels to manage. He wanted to start small and gear up slowly as he built up more internally generated revenues.

Craig started to list the types of businesses he thought he might be successful at.

4. What are the barriers to entry for this industry?

Some industries are more difficult than others to "break into." For an extreme example, it would be incredibly difficult to start up a new auto manufacturing company to compete with Ford or Daimler Chrysler. Likewise, it would be almost impossible to set up a new company to provide telephone service to the Eastern seaboard. In both of these examples, the start-up costs are monumental (design, manufacturing equipment, and showrooms in the first instance and switching stations and telephone cabling in the second). Also, these industries are dominated by a few very large players who have built name recognition and goodwill over many years.

Ensure that you choose an industry where there is room for new participants to grow.

5. Can the business weather downturns?

Every industry has up and down times. For example, travel agents book more vacations for their customers when the economy is on an upswing than when it's in recession. A business can also be affected by how many new businesses in that industry are opening up. A flood of new providers can siphon off some of your customers, at least in the short term.

Look at whether the business you are contemplating will be able to survive external changes to its operating environment. Is your product or service easily adaptable? For example, in poor economic times, a spa will focus on advertising the basic services, such as haircuts. When times are good, it will promote higher-end services, such as massage, facials, and pedicures.

6. How easily can I expand this business?

If your goal is to grow your business over several years, it's critical to determine upfront whether the business has the potential to do

that. For example, if you start a grocery store in a small town, your customer base is limited to the residents of the town. You may find it difficult to grow such a business without offering new products.

Ensure that the business has the potential to grow quickly and expand either the customer base or the range of products or services.

7. Will my product or service endure?

The only constant in business is the knowledge that consumer tastes are ever changing. The product that may have been all the rage last month may be passé this month. Think back to pet rocks, fruit-flavored potato chips, and Rubik's Cube. These items sold extremely well for an extremely short period of time. If you had built your business around one of these fads, however, you would soon have found revenues dropping precipitously and you would have been out of business quickly (unless, of course, your business hopped from fad to fad).

It's important to make sure that your service or product is not a fad and will be needed long into the future.

8. Will I actually be able to make money with this business?

If you feel that you have found an under-serviced market niche, you need to examine why there are no other businesses serving that market. Many small businesses are able to create a toehold in an industry because large corporations would not be able to make enough profit serving that market to satisfy their investors. A small business has the advantage of lower overhead and more flexibility to move in and out of markets and can often create greater profits than its larger counterparts. However, if you want to do more than simply eke out a living running your business, make sure that the profit potential is there right from the beginning.

Chapter Summary

➡ In order to start and run a small business by yourself, you need to have skills in business building, business management, and doing what the business does.

➡ There are three main types of businesses: manufacturing, retail/wholesale, and service. When deciding what type of business to start, it's important to look at the pros and cons of running each type of business.

➡ Ensure that your personal goals fit with your plans for your business with respect to finances, freedom, and risk.

➡ It is critical to examine your choice of potential business to make sure that the product or service is viable and will stand the test of time.

Is It a Business or a Hobby?

How do you know whether your interests will produce monetary returns? We look at decision planning for your great idea.

Introduction

It's inevitable. If you're a true entrepreneur, you will eventually begin to analyze every possible venture to see if it would make a viable business. You will look at your spouse's scrapbooking project and think about the possibility of opening a scrapbooking store. You will think about ways to leverage your son's after-school lawn-cutting venture to provide service to twice the customers at half the price. When a kind-hearted jogger in the park comments on how she wishes she had a dog, you will mentally calculate how many times you would have to rent out Fido to "dogless" people to break even.

Entrepreneurs are always thinking about business. It's what sets them apart from other people and makes them visionary. There is, however, the dark side of the moon where ventures that are pure hobby are turned into businesses that are doomed to fail. It's critical to be able to tell the difference between a business and a hobby. Just because you love to go fly-fishing doesn't mean that you can make money at it.

Many highly successful entrepreneurs build and invest in businesses without having any personal interest in what the business does. They are only concerned about what growth potential the business has and its profitability. Think about Warren Buffett and Donald Trump. But there are other small-business owners who have parlayed a personal interest or hobby into a highly successful business. These business owners have, however, conducted the same analysis of the business potential as have the Buffetts and Trumps of the world. They have realized that something they enjoy doing has the potential to be a thriving business enterprise. That is not so, however, with all hobbies.

What Is the Difference Between a Business and a Hobby?

Let's look at the characteristics of a business versus a hobby.

Characteristics of a business:

- Designed on sound business principles
- Tailored to the needs of its customers
- Enjoyment garnered from building or managing the business
- Reasonable expectation of increasing profit over time

Characteristics of a hobby:

- Tailored to the needs of the hobbyist
- Incurs high costs compared to potential return
- Designed based on desires of the hobbyist
- Enjoyment garnered from performing the service
- Little or no expectation of increasing profits over time

A sound business is always centered on its customers. The reason for its existence is to serve its customer base, and customer satisfaction is the measure of its success. An entrepreneur who builds and manages a small business derives his or her pleasure from the *process* of providing the product or service as opposed to the actual provision.

Let's use a deep sea diving outfit to demonstrate the difference between a business and a hobby. Maria owns a boat and several sets of dive gear. She has been doing deep sea diving almost all of her life and she wants to take

---

CASE STUDY

The first idea Craig came up with for his new business was operating a taxi service. He had driven a taxi part time when he was in college and he knew a lot about the business. He had even helped the taxi service's owner develop new routing procedures to lessen the drivers' down time. After drawing up some preliminary plans, however, Craig realized that owning a taxi service would violate two of his personal goals: having a balanced work/family life and not having a huge up-front investment. A taxi service would require a strong hands-on manager and he would have to fill that role until he could find someone to replace him. It also would require the purchase or lease of a central dispatch office as well as several cars. His estimates showed that he would be working approximately 60 hours per week on average and would have to find an initial investment of $120,000. He decided to leave the taxi business to someone else.

The next business opportunity Craig investigated was cheese-making. Craig had a passion for cheese-making that dated back to his days at his father's bakery. His father's brother, his Uncle Nino, had been the cheese-maker in the family. He ran a small cheese shop next door to the bakery for almost as long as Craig's father had run the bakery. Craig had worked at the bakery out of duty to his father, but he loved the occasional opportunity he got to work with his Uncle Nino making cheese. They made hard cheeses like Parmesan and Romano, and soft ones like Brie and Gouda. Craig still made cheese for his wife in a small basement room.

It made sense to Craig that he start a business based on a skill he was good at and loved. He quickly came to realize, however, that he was following the same path as his father, without the assurance of success. High-quality cheeses appealed only to a small segment of the market, and Craig would once again have to be at the business all the time as he was the one with the skill to produce the cheese. Rather reluctantly, Craig shelved the idea of building a cheese-making empire.

others out to teach them how to do it. If this is simply a hobby for Maria, she will take people out to dive sites that she particularly enjoys and will purchase dive equipment and other supplies without regard to analyzing the cost versus the benefit of such expenditures. She will set hours that are convenient to her and will only book tours during that time. The enjoyment that she gets is in the actual diving itself. She wants to share her hobby with others and has no interest in hiring others to perform the work or in growing or selling the business.

On the other hand, if this is a true business, Maria will spend time upfront "crunching the numbers": calculating her break-even point by figuring out how many tours she needs to book to cover the capital cost of the boat and its related maintenance, as well as the dive equipment. She will research what tourists are most interested in when they book a diving tour and will adjust her availability to the most popular tourist seasons. If the growth potential is present to allow it, she will most likely hire another experienced diver in order to be able to run more tours. The enjoyment that Maria will get from building this business is in seeing it grow and serve its customers. She will know that she is building something that will outlast her and that she can sell when she wants to pursue other ventures.

It's definitely true that many successful entrepreneurs have translated their personal interests into highly successful businesses, and potentially, you can too. However, it's always important to make sure that your reasons for starting the business extend beyond the pure enjoyment of doing what the business does.

It's Not Always about the Money

Now that we've discussed why you should be extremely careful in trying to make your hobby your business, it's important to make the point that you can still have a hobby. Not everything you do has to produce profit. In fact, the most fun part about a hobby is that you do not have to worry about things like profitability or the satisfaction of others. Trying to turn your hobby into a business may not only be unprofitable, but may also make you end up hating the hobby. Entrepreneurs and small-business owners need to have more interests than just their businesses in order to maintain a balanced lifestyle. If you do nothing except keep your nose to the grindstone in your business all day, everyday, think about what an uninteresting person you'd be!

Chapter Summary

➡ Entrepreneurs are continually assessing potential ventures to see if they would make profitable businesses, but they run the risk of trying to turn a purely pleasurable pastime into an unprofitable business.

➡ Although many successful small-business owners have parlayed their personal interests into successful businesses, many more build and grow a business without a personal interest in the underlying activities of the business.

➡ Businesses are always run for the benefit of the customers, whereas hobbies are undertaken for the benefit of the hobbyist.

➡ Small-business owners should still pursue hobbies and personal interests to maintain a balance between their personal and business lives.

Build or Buy?

Is it better to build a business from the ground up or to purchase an existing business? This chapter outlines the considerations.

Introduction

If you want to become a small-business owner, there are two ways to do it: you can either build a business from the ground up or you can buy an existing business. Each strategy has its pros and cons. The strategy that's right for you will depend partly on your motivation for being a small-business owner and partly on cash flow considerations.

If your motivation for starting a small business is that you derive pleasure from building something from nothing, you are more likely to garner that pleasure from building your own business, although you may also take pleasure in buying a business and molding it into your image. On the other hand, your interests may lie more on the managing side and you would therefore prefer to walk into an existing business and begin to run it.

Cash flow also plays a part in your decision. If you are purchasing goodwill along with the net assets of the business, you will be paying more than if you simply purchase assets and start from scratch. Buying an existing business is usually the more expensive option. However, a business that is already up and running may provide you with profits and a management income earlier. This may offset the initial cost. When you build a small business from scratch, it may take months or even a year before you hit the break-even point, much less make profit that you can put in your pocket. In the meantime, you will be investing a large amount of your time building the enterprise without remuneration, and this is a cost that you must figure into your calculations as well.

Let's look at the pros and cons of building a business from scratch versus those of buying an existing business.

13

Building a Business from Scratch

When you build a business from scratch, you will start with nothing but the tiniest grain of an idea. You will spend months or longer mapping out that idea, running cash flow scenarios, doing market and competitive analysis, writing a business plan and a management operating plan, and working on the business's vision and mission statements. You will be meeting with bankers, accountants, lawyers, and financial planners as you build your external advisory team.

You will most likely open your doors before you take in the first dollar in revenues, and you will take the enormous leap of faith that customers will actually want what you are selling the way you had it laid out in the plan.

It sounds scary but designing and building the business that exists in your head can be an extremely fulfilling and gratifying experience. So much so, that many successful entrepreneurs design and build businesses, then sell them once they're up and running. Then they start all over again and build another one.

Here are some of the pros of building a business from scratch:

CASE STUDY

It was then that the perfect business quite literally fell into Craig's lap. It was his second wedding anniversary and he had taken his wife out for dinner at an upscale French bistro. As they were enjoying their desserts, the power went out, an occurrence that was becoming all too common on the Eastern seaboard where they lived.

There were auxiliary lights in the bistro, just enough for Craig to see most of the patrons leaving, despite the servers' quick efforts to light candles on every table. The server looking after Craig and Marnie's table told them that some were leaving because they were uncomfortable with the blackout and some because the bistro couldn't accept credit cards because its system worked solely on electricity. Craig sipped his wine and contemplated the money that the restaurant was losing because of the blackout, when, quite unexpectedly, the busboy tripped in the aisle and dumped a half-eaten plate of gnocchi in Craig's lap.

"I'm so sorry," the busboy said, cleaning up the mess. "I couldn't see where I was going. I hate these blackouts."

Craig wondered aloud to Marnie how many businesses were facing the same problem at that moment along the Seaboard. Business was being lost because of the lights not being on. Craig then recalled an article he had recently read in the paper about a new company called Green Power Inc. that was selling solar and wind energy solutions to both businesses and residences. Craig hadn't given much thought to the concept until now, but suddenly realized the benefits to both business owners and homeowners.

The next morning (several hours after the lights came back on), Craig called Green Power Inc. to find out more information. Craig met with the owner that afternoon and, two weeks later, Craig was presented with an offer to buy into a new offshoot of Green Power Inc. aimed at the residential market. Craig would have a 50 percent ownership stake in the new business with Gordon, the current owner of Green Power. Craig's responsibilities would be those of the general manager; he would run the day-to-day operations and would head up all strategic and operational planning. For this, he would be paid a salary of $67,000 plus would receive dividends as an owner of the company.

Craig spent the following week with his accountant, analyzing the offer and the potential return. He compared it to the cost of starting up his own alternative energy company and determined that the cost of starting from scratch would outweigh the additional profit from owning the entire business. He would not only have to invest in all of the marketing materials, but he would have to develop the necessary expertise in alternative energy. Craig's best opportunity would be to buy into the new offshoot of the existing company.

- You can design internal systems the way you want them to work right from the beginning.
- It can be less expensive than buying an existing operation.
- There is no risk of acquiring the previous owners' liabilities or having to satisfy pre-existing warranties.
- You can manage staffing needs more carefully (i.e., you don't inherit employees that are sub-par and/or difficult to fire).

There are some cons to building a business from scratch:

- It can be more difficult and expensive to attract investors. Because the venture doesn't exist yet, it will be riskier for them.
- It can take longer to generate profits than with an existing business.
- It can take a long time to build name recognition and goodwill with customers.
- There is a much greater risk of failure than with a business that has a proven track record.

Buying an Existing Business

Buying an existing business is, in general, less of a risk for you as the major investor. You have the opportunity to watch the business in action and you will be able to access the historical financial information to determine patterns such as growth rate, profitability, and solvency. You know that you will be able to generate a return on your investment almost immediately as well as be remunerated for your management role in the business (and perhaps also your operational role).

You may also choose to buy a business if you want to quickly introduce a new product to an existing customer base before there are too many competitors in the market. For example, if you have developed a brand new print-on-demand self-serve book station, you may want to have instant access to a thriving bookstore's customers before copycats come on the market.

Here are some of the pros of buying an existing business:

- It can be easier to obtain external financing than if you build a business from scratch because the business has a track record.
- You can market your existing products to a new customer base.
- It is easier to manage an existing business model and fine-tune it than build it from the ground up.
- You can generate profits right from the purchase date.
- You can continue the business with the existing goodwill and name recognition.

There are some cons to buying an existing business:

- You may be inheriting the hidden headaches of the previous owner.
- You may be inheriting "negative goodwill" if the business had a bad name in the community.
- It may take as long to reshape the business the way you want it as it would to have started a new business from scratch.
- The customers you are "buying" may have only been loyal to the former owner and may choose not to stay on as customers when you take over.

Financial Considerations in the Build-versus-Buy Decision

Once you have taken into consideration your personal goals and your tolerance of risk, the decision to buy versus build a business comes down to a financial one. There are many ways to analyze a purchase decision, but we will look at the most common: the discounted cash flow method.

Discounted cash flow analysis (DCF) helps us to look at a purchase decision and figure out at what point our cash inflows (revenue) match and then exceed our cash outflows (operating and financing costs). DCF takes into consideration the important fact that the timing of the inflows and outflows of cash are different. A dollar received three years from now is worth less than a dollar that we have to spend today. This is called the time value of money and is the basis of DCF analysis. For more information on cash flows, please refer to *Financial Management 101,* the second book in the *Numbers 101 for Small Business* series.

Let's look at an example to see DCF in action:

You have been offered the opportunity to purchase a sign-making company for $225,000. You have already talked to your bank manager and she is willing to finance $175,000 but you will have to use $50,000 of your own savings to finance the rest. You have been thinking about starting up a similar type of company for some time and you want to compare the cash flows of purchasing an existing business versus building one from scratch.

Considering a start-up business

You have put together a cash flow projection for the proposed start-up company. The five-year cash flow projection is shown in Sample 1.

In this start-up company, you would be investing $50,000 of your own money in order to finance the start-up costs of $18,860 and the cash shortfalls in years one and two ($17,060 and $7,250 respectively). By year three, the company is projected to have a cash surplus, which grows annually up to year five.

You can see that before you even open the doors, you will have to invest $18,860 into the company. Most of that money goes towards buying the sign-making equipment and inventory. Further investments in equipment will have to be made every year as the company starts increasing sales.

How can we evaluate whether or not this option would be a sound investment? There are many methods of decision analysis. The method we'll consider here is to look at discounted cash flows. This method allows us to come up with an annualized return on investment. Remember that you will invest $50,000 into this venture. You could have taken that $50,000 and put it in the stock market or invested it in bonds. Both of those activities would have generated a return. In the same manner, we can look at the return from this start-up business.

The annualized return on investment is simply the amount of funds left over to put in the owners' pocket after all of the business expenses are paid. Note that we are talking about *all* the expenses, which includes remuneration for all work done in the business. In this scenario, you will be paid a management salary of $48,000 in years one and two, $59,000 in years three and four, and $63,000 in year five.

If, however, your cash flow projections don't allow for you to be paid for your labor, calculating a return on investment is rather

SAMPLE 1
CASH FLOW PROJECTION FOR A START-UP BUSINESS

	On start up	Year 1	Year 2	Year 3	Year 4	Year 5
Cash receipts		163,000	197,000	259,000	375,000	425,000
Inventory purchases	4,965	70,090	84,710	111,370	161,250	182,750
Advertising		7,950	7,275	6,950	6,750	6,750
Bank charges		1,250	1,250	1,250	1,250	1,250
Office expenses		5,310	6,150	7,630	10,995	11,865
Professional fees	1,275	2,200	2,400	2,600	2,950	3,250
Rent	2,000	24,000	25,350	27,695	48,000	50,050
Supplies	975	6,000	6,500	7,100	7,640	7,950
Telephone & utilities	395	3,600	3,75	4,150	6,525	6,750
Vehicle expenses		2,400	2,640	2,980	4,525	4,745
Management salary		48,000	48,000	59,000	59,000	63,000
Wages & benefits		6,515	13,225	15,000	32,000	36,500
Purchase of capital equipment	9,250	2,745	3,000	3,625	8,525	3,750
Total inflows	-	163,000	197,000	259,000	375,000	425,000
Total outflows	18,860	180,060	204,250	249,350	349,410	378,610
Net cash inflows (outflows)	(18,860)	(17,060)	(7,250)	9,650	25,590	46,390
Total invested by owner		50,000				
Annualized ROI		5.27%				

meaningless. It means that, not only are you investing money, you are investing your labor for free (this is known as "sweat equity"). In this scenario, however, you are being paid for your efforts and therefore can look at how much you're getting for your $50,000 investment.

The net cash available for distribution to the owners looks like this:

On start up	($18,860)
Year 1	(17,060)
Year 2	(7,250)
Year 3	9,650
(YEA!! Positive cash flow!)	
Year 4	25,590
Year 5	46,390

We also know from the above discussion that a dollar received or spent tomorrow is worth less than a dollar received or spent today. This means that we will want to discount this stream of cash flows back to today, to the present value of the dollar, to make sure we are comparing apples to apples, so to speak. The first thing that we need to do is to find a meaningful interest rate at which to discount the cash flows. After speaking with your banker, you know that you can borrow from the bank at 10 percent, so we will use this rate to do our discounting. There is a formula to calculate the present value of a dollar, but we will take the easy way and use a table. This table is found in Appendix 1. Match the interest rate (in this case, 10 percent) at the top with the periods along the side, and read off the corresponding factor for each period. To calculate how much your future cash flows are worth today, multiply each cash flow by the factor for that period.

Let's follow through the example, using a portion of the present value table reproduced below:

Period	10%
1	0.9091
2	0.8264
3	0.7513
4	0.6830
5	0.6209

This table tells us, for example, that if we are going to receive a dollar a year from now, it is only really worth 90.91¢ today. You can see that, as we go farther into the future, the worth of that same dollar becomes less and less. We have to bring all of our cash flows back to a common point: today. Sample 2 has completed the calculations.

This tells us that, over five years, the company will generate $13,171 in net positive discounted cash flow. We also know that you will have to invest $50,000 to get that cash flow. The calculation for your average annualized return on investment (ROI) is:

ROI = net cash flow ÷ investment ÷ # years

Therefore, your ROI in this scenario will be:

ROI = 13,171 ÷ 50,000 ÷ 5 = 5.27%

Your average annual return on your initial investment is 5.27 percent. This calculation is helpful in deciding whether to invest the money in this business or another business or another type of investment altogether. It is important to realize, however, that after year five, the cash flow is in permanently better position as the company matures. Therefore, by the time year six rolls around, the business will be generating in excess of $46,000 in net profit; a much higher return for the initial investment. Return on investment analysis will change depending on the time frame used.

Considering a business purchase

Let's look at the cash flows for the projected business purchase and see how they compare to the start-up business using the same analysis.

SAMPLE 2
DISCOUNTED CASH FLOWS FOR A START-UP BUSINESS

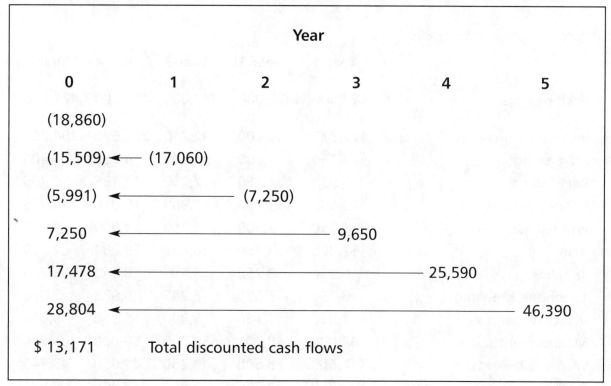

The purchase price for the business is $225,000. The bank is willing to lend $175,000 at 10 percent and you will have to invest $50,000 of your own money. This company has been in business for many years and therefore has mature cash flows already, similar to those in your projections for year five of the start-up company. The cash flow projections are shown in Sample 3.

There are a few important items to note here:

- The purchase of capital equipment is more regular than in the build scenario and of similar amounts from year to year. The company already owns its equipment (that's part of what you're buying) but some will need to be replaced

every year as it wears out or becomes obsolete.

- The revenues are growing by a lesser percentage than with the start-up company. This company already has a mature market and grows at a slower pace than a business in its infancy.

- The net cash flow of the business operations is much higher than that of the start-up, but we have to figure in the payments of principal and interest on the bank loan before we can calculate the return on the owner's investment.

- In both scenarios (start-up and purchase), the management salary is the same and therefore does not become a factor in the decision-making process.

SAMPLE 3
CASH FLOW PROJECTION FOR A BUSINESS PURCHASE

Purchase price = $225,000

	Year 1	Year 2	Year 3	Year 4	Year 5
Cash receipts	412,500	420,000	447,000	464,000	471,500
Inventory purchases	177,375	180,600	192,210	201,670	204,250
Advertising	4,150	4,200	4,200	4,350	4,400
Bank charges	1,950	1,950	2,050	2,195	2,235
Office expenses	12,540	13,250	13,985	15,010	15,775
Professional fees	3,250	3,500	3,750	4,000	4,250
Rent	52,000	53,750	56,450	59,000	62,450
Supplies	8,250	8,250	8,495	8,540	8,725
Telephone & utilities	6,250	6,550	6,745	6,985	7,140
Vehicle expenses	4,950	5,150	5,300	5,350	5,615
Management salary	48,000	48,000	59,000	59,000	63,000
Wages & benefits	37,500	38,500	40,250	41,950	43,745
Purchase of capital equipment	3,750	3,750	3,895	3,895	3,975
Interest on line of credit	-	-	-	-	-
Total inflows	412,500	420,000	447,000	464,000	471,500
Total outflows	359,965	367,450	396,330	411,945	425,560
Net cash inflows/(outflows)	52,535	52,550	50,670	52,055	45,940
Interest & principal payments	44,620	44,620	44,620	44,620	44,620
Net return to owner	7,915	7,930	6,050	7,435	1,320
Total invested by owner	50,000				
Annualized ROI	9.68%				

However, if the salaries in each were different, you would have to "normalize" them. This means that you would have to recast the numbers of one or the other (or both!) projections to reflect the amount of management salary that you intend to take from the business, otherwise you are not comparing apples to apples.

Take a look at the discounted cash flows for the purchased business in Sample 4.

This tells us that the total discounted cash flows of $24,192 are higher than in the start-up scenario ($13,171). However, if the amount of the original investment had been more in the purchase scenario, this still may not be the better option. The only way to accurately compare between the two is to complete the ROI calculation. In the purchase scenario, the calculation works out to:

ROI = net cash flow ÷ investment ÷ # years

ROI = 24,192 ÷ 50,000 ÷ 5 = 9.68%

The option to purchase the existing business yields a return on your $50,000 investment of 9.68 percent, while the start-up would only yield 5.27 percent. All other things being equal, purchasing the existing business makes more financial sense.

Just to reinforce the concepts, try calculating the ROI analysis if all cash flows were the same but you had to invest $95,000 to purchase the existing business. Would this be the better option? The answer is no. If you have to invest $95,000 of your own money to purchase this business, the ROI drops from 9.68 percent

SAMPLE 4
DISCOUNTED CASH FLOWS FOR A BUSINESS PURCHASE

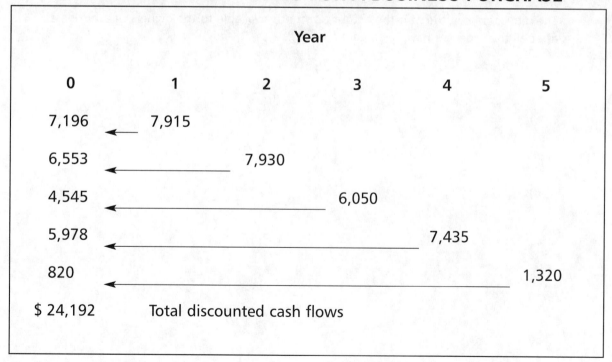

	Year				
0	1	2	3	4	5
7,196	7,915				
6,553		7,930			
4,545			6,050		
5,978				7,435	
820					1,320
$ 24,192	Total discounted cash flows				

to 5 percent, thereby giving you less reward for a higher risk than starting a business from scratch.

What's Right for You?

As we have discussed in this chapter, there are many considerations when you are deciding whether to start a business from scratch or to purchase an existing business. Many of those considerations relate back to your personal and business goals and will be determined by the reasons that you want to be a business owner in the first place. You will need to balance those goals with solid financial analysis to determine which option will give you the best opportunity for success.

Chapter Summary

➡ Building a business, managing a business, and working in a business are three very different activities and it is important that you analyze which ones are most important to you before you start any business.

➡ The two ways to become a business owner are to build a business from scratch or to buy an existing business. Each has its own pros and cons.

➡ Calculating the discounted cash flows of each business option will ensure that you are properly comparing future cash flows with each other.

➡ The return on investment is the amount of funds available to the owners of a business after all the expenses have been paid.

Chapter

4

Getting Your Personal Finances in Order

Before you start your business, you need to make sure that the rest of your financial house is in order.

Introduction

One of your personal goals may be to make enough money out of your business to be wealthy, or at least be comfortable. You may see starting a small business as a way out of your current financial woes. This is a very dangerous way of thinking. You are likely to manage your business the same way you manage your personal life. If you have problems managing personal debt, that may be true in your business as well. If you don't know how much insurance you need to cover off your personal assets, you may under-insure your business assets and unknowingly be exposed to risk.

It is important to clean up your own financial house before you start or buy a business. A bank will undoubtedly review your personal financial situation before lending the business any money. Suppliers who extend your business credit may also want to review your credit history and personal wealth. Your personal financial situation might end up crippling your business's ability to attract investment capital. From a more practical perspective, if you don't have your personal financial life under control now, where will you find the time to do so while building your business empire?

Integrating your personal financial planning into your business planning gives you a more holistic and global view of your entire financial life and will help you to define your financial and retirement goals.

Your Retirement Goals

So you've decided to jump into the role of entrepreneur. You have fantastic vision and insight and are looking forward to managing and growing your business for a long time to come. Have you thought about what happens then? Do you still plan on coming into the office every day at 9 a.m. when you're 60? 70? How about 90? Most likely, you have at least a vague concept of what you want to do when you're older. You may even have decided that you want to make enough money in your business to retire when you're 40 or 50.

Analyzing your retirement goals involves more than just vague concepts. It is the basis for your business and personal financial plans. If you're planning that your business will provide you a steady income for your working life and then a small gain on sale when you sell, you need to ensure that these funds will be sufficient to meet your financial needs when you retire, otherwise, you'll need to keep working longer than you had anticipated.

The minimum financial goal for your retirement is to be financially independent. Financial independence means that you will be able to live off your financial capital for the rest of your life without working, if you wish.

Let's look at an example to illustrate how this works. We will walk through a simple example, which will exclude some complexities that exist in real life, like the impact of taxes and income from other sources such as pensions. When you are making your retirement calculations, I highly recommend that you do so with the assistance of your accountant or independent financial adviser (by independent, I mean someone who doesn't make commissions from the products he or she sells you).

Start by getting a handle on how much income you need per year to live on after you have retired. Keep in mind that you will have

---

CASE STUDY

Craig and Marnie discussed the implications of being business owners. Craig was looking forward to the adventure but Marnie had some reservations.

"We still have so much credit card debt. I doubt the bank will lend us the money we need to buy into this business."

"Why don't we go talk to the bank about consolidating our credit cards?" said Craig. "We have some equity in the house that we're not using so maybe the bank can help us out."

The next day, Craig met with his accountant, Vivian. Vivian confirmed Marnie's suspicions that they needed to rearrange some of their personal finances before they could approach a bank or another lender for funding to purchase the business.

Vivian recommended that they increase their mortgage to be able to pay off their revolving debt, namely, their credit cards.

"Lowering your revolving debt will increase your credit score," Vivian said, "and that will make a bank more likely to lend you some of the capital you will need to invest in this business."

Craig was more confident than ever that he was going to be able to buy into this business, but Vivian brought up some other issues that he hadn't thought about.

"What will happen if you can't work in the business? How will you support Marnie and the baby?" Vivian asked.

Craig hadn't thought about this before. He scheduled an appointment for the next day with his insurance agent to ensure that he would have adequate coverage for any adversity that may arise.

(hopefully!) no debt or mortgage payment and that your assets will be owned free and clear. You will simply have your ongoing living expenses (e.g., property taxes, utilities, food, clothing, medical) and any money that you need to carry out your retirement dreams, such as travel costs. Your post-retirement income needs are likely to be much lower than your current ones. Let's say that you have decided that you want to have $50,000 per year to live on when you retire. You are 35 right now and plan on retiring when you are 60. Therefore you have 25 years to save for your retirement. You want to make sure that you are being conservative and plan to live until you are 90 years old, so you will need the $50,000 per year for 30 years. You have life insurance and therefore have no need to have any cash left at death. There are two questions that need to be answered mathematically:

- How much will you need to have saved by the time you are 60 in order to meet your income requirements? and

- How much will you have to put into your retirement fund each year between now and age 60 to have that amount available?

We will use a 6 percent average return for our calculations.

How much will you need at age 60?

This is simply a mathematical calculation that involves the present value of an annuity. The full table used for the calculation is in Appendix 2. To calculate, you multiply the annual income required ($50,000) by the appropriate factor in the table. Multiplying by this factor takes into account the fact that future dollars are not worth as much as today's dollars. At an interest rate of 6 percent and 30 annual periods, the factor is 13.765. Therefore, the amount that you need to have in retirement savings by the time you are 60 is $50,000 x 13.765 = $688,250. In most cases, this won't have to come solely from savings. You may have pension income from a job or a 401K. Your business will also likely have a value when you sell it to retire. Be careful about making these assumptions too rosy in case they don't happen. In this scenario, we will assume that the entire retirement fund is coming from savings.

How much do you have to put away between now and retirement?

You know that you will need $688,250 by the time you turn 60. You have 25 years to save that amount (at an assumed 6 percent rate of return). How much will you have to sock away every year to meet your goal? Again, the formula is simple mathematics. We now use the future value of an annuity to calculate the payments. The full table is reproduced in Appendix 3. Using a 6 percent interest rate and 25 periods, the factor is 54.865. You divide the required retirement fund amount by the factor to come up with the annual payments into the fund. In this case, it is $688,250 ÷ 54.865 = $12,544 per year that you will have to tuck into your retirement fund in order to meet your retirement goals.

So, why is this information important to you now, when you are starting up your business? It's important when you set your business financial goals. You now know that if you want to meet your personal retirement goals, you will have to draw enough from your business not only to cover your current living expenses, but also an extra $12,544 per year to fund your retirement. Many small-business owners have retirement goals that are at odds with what they are making from their businesses. The earlier you integrate these goals, the more likely you will achieve them.

Use the template in Worksheet 1 to begin to contemplate your own retirement goals.

The Concept of Net Wealth

How much are you really worth? You may be drawing a large salary from your business but if it all gets spent on current expenses, it doesn't add to the value of your possessions. One of the most important measures in your personal financial planning is your net wealth. This is simply your assets minus your liabilities. Over time, your assets should grow and your liabilities should decrease, which decreases the risks you are exposed to and increases your financial stability. Ultimately, your net wealth is what you have to live on and then to pass on to the next generation.

It doesn't have to be onerous to track your net wealth. You can simply write down your best estimate of the value of all of your assets and then the payout amount of all of your liabilities (i.e., the amount of money it would take to settle up your debts). You may also choose to use a software program that will track not only your net wealth but also your income and spending. It may also track your retirement savings. Popular programs such as Intuit's *Quicken* or *Microsoft Money* make the tracking easy. If you do this on a regular basis (monthly or at least annually) you will be able to see how your wealth increases over time.

Your assets may include:
- Cash
- Portfolio investments (bonds, stocks, etc.)
- Your home
- Other real estate (cottages, vacant land, rental properties, etc.)
- Vehicles
- Savings (including retirement accounts and college funds)
- Your business

Your liabilities may include:
- Mortgage
- Credit card balances
- Personal loans
- Car loan

The higher your net wealth, the more likely a bank will look favorably upon your business as it needs financing.

Debt Management

In order to make sure that you will manage your business debt appropriately, it's important to first get a handle on your personal debt.

There is an old adage about good debt versus bad debt. Bad debt is defined as any debt you undertake to purchase things that do not grow in value. This would apply if you're using your credit card or line of credit to go on a vacation or buy living room furniture or a car. Good debt, on the other hand, is debt that's incurred to invest in things that will grow in value, such as your home, other real estate, and stock market investments. Conventional wisdom says that bad debt should be avoided or paid down as quickly as possible, but good debt is acceptable and should even be pursued.

The problem with this outlook is that it does not recognize that debt means risk for you, regardless of what that debt buys you. Any time you have required payments to make, you run the risk of not being able to pay them and thereby becoming insolvent or even bankrupt. When you borrow to invest, either in real estate or in bonds or the stock market, there is no guarantee that these investments will increase in the short term, which is when you have to make the payments. There is a danger that, if the value of the investment drops below what is owed on the loan, the loan will be called. In that situation, even if the investment is sold, you will still owe money.

WORKSHEET 1
RETIREMENT PLANNING

A. Current age: _____

B. Planned retirement age: _____

C. Years to retirement (B minus A): _____

D. Expected life span in years: _____

E. No. of years retirement income required (D minus B): _____

F. Amount of annual income required at retirement: _____

G. Estimated annual return on investment: _____

H. Factor from table in Appendix 3 using rate in (G) and no. years in (E): _____

I. Income in (F) multiplied by factor in (H): _____ Amount needed

J. Factor from table in Appendix 4 using rate in (G) and no. years in (C): _____

K. Amount from (I) divided by factor in (J): _____ Amount to fund per year

Another investment "nugget" suggests that paying interest on investment loans in order to build investment assets is a good idea. As we have discussed above, all investment entails risk, whereas paying down your debts can give you a greater return on an after-tax basis. Let's look at an example:

Your spouse has received a $5,000 bonus from his employer. You are considering whether to invest that in your investment account or to pay off the last of your credit card debt. Currently, the long-term investment return from stock investments is about 6 percent. You will have to pay taxes on part of that income, however, and therefore, your after-tax return may be as low as 3 or 4 percent. On the other hand, your credit card company charges 19 percent. Paying off that card will give you a 19 percent return after tax, as there are no tax implications of paying off debt. Not only is your return much higher, paying off debt gives you that return risk free. It's a guaranteed return. Always keep this in mind when trying to decide what to do with windfalls and extra money in your budget.

I'm certainly not advocating that you do not have any personal debt whatsoever. Simply keep in mind that debt equals risk. As a small-business owner, you will be exposed to plenty of risk as it is, without adding to it on the personal side. Here are some things that you can do to get a handle on your personal debt situation:

1. List out all of your personal debts, the terms left on them, and the interest rate.

2. Rank your debts by highest to lowest interest rates. You will find that the highest interest rate debts are generally credit cards, retail cards, rent-to-own situations, and payday loans. The more the debt is secured by underlying assets, the lower the rate will be. For example, because the bank can take back your home if you do not make the mortgage payments, mortgage rates tend to be lower because the risk to the bank (not to you!) is lower.

3. Review your budget and calculate how much you can set aside for debt repayment.

4. Make a formal debt repayment plan. For each debt, you should know how long it will take to pay off (not just the minimum required by the lender). Start with the highest interest rate debts and pay them off as quickly as possible.

5. Stick to your budget! Make sure that you make the payments that you have calculated every month in order to be out of debt when you have planned to be.

Your Credit History

In North America, almost every person who has ever borrowed money from an institution will have a credit report on file with one of the major credit bureaus. This report will have your borrowing and employment history, including amounts owing, how quickly you have repaid past loans, whether any payments are overdue, and whether a lender has ever had to turn any of your debt over to a collection agency in the past. Any past bankruptcies will also show up on this report. This information culminates in your credit score, which is used by lenders to predict whether or not you are a good credit risk. Having a poor score can not only ensure that you are denied future credit but you may also have to pay a much higher interest rate to offset what the lender perceives as your increased risk.

You have a right to have access to your own credit reports and it is highly recommended that you review it on a regular basis, as often as yearly. It's important for you to know how a future lender will view you. There is also the possibility that your credit report contains inaccurate information, which you should have corrected as soon as possible to avoid it impacting your credit-worthiness.

Your personal credit history will also come into play when you start your small business. Most banks and leasing companies will check your personal credit score to make sure that you pay both your personal and business debts on time. This will matter greatly when you apply for a business line of credit or for a lease arrangement for your equipment.

Make sure your personal credit history is as clean and in order as possible before you contemplate starting your business. It will save you many headaches down the road.

In the United States, there are three national credit reporting agencies for individuals and it is important to see your credit information from all three:

- Equifax: www.equifax.com
- TransUnion: www.transunion.com
- Experian: www.experian.com

In Canada, there are two national reporting agencies:

- Equifax: www.equifax.com
- TransUnion: www.tuc.ca

Insuring Your Assets

Insurance isn't a topic that many people give much thought to. But it goes hand-in-hand with our discussion about risk. In its most simple terms, insurance (for a fee) protects us against the risk of losing our assets. As a small-business owner, having adequate insurance

will become vitally important. Let's have a look at the major categories of insurance that you should consider.

Life insurance

What will happen when you die? Basically, anyone who is dependent upon you bringing in income will no longer have that source of income. This will be especially important if you have a spouse and children. The family home must still be maintained and the children's education accounts must still be funded. It may be impossible for your spouse to carry the burden alone when you are gone. If this is the case, it's imperative that you have life insurance to replace your lost income, at least until the children are grown and self-sufficient. If, however, you are single and have no other dependents, life insurance is not a necessity and the premiums that you would otherwise pay might be better off in an investment account.

There are many types of life insurance, some of which have an investment component to them. A discussion of the options available is beyond the scope of this book and should be discussed with your accountant or independent financial adviser.

How much life insurance do you need? You should be able to review your current spending budget and compare it to the after-tax income of your spouse (remember that he or she will most likely keep working). The shortfall between the expenses and the income will need to be funded through life insurance. Another alternative is to insure for the amount of your debts, including your mortgage. Then, upon your death, your spouse will only have to pay ongoing living expenses and not have any debt payments.

Mortgage insurance

Mortgage insurance will pay off the outstanding balance of your mortgage when you die.

However, the premiums for most policies are set based on the amount owing when the policy is set up. So, for example, you may owe $150,000 now on your mortgage and will pay premiums based on that. In ten years, when you die, you may only owe $10,000 and that would be the amount paid out on the policy. In general, the premiums for mortgage insurance tend to be high compared to the payout. Mortgage insurance can be replaced with additional life insurance for a much lower cost in many cases, and should be discussed with your accountant or independent financial planner.

Property and casualty insurance

This type of insurance protects you from the loss of your belongings, such as your house and its contents, your car, and any other physical assets you may have. Many property and casualty policies also contain a liability component, so that, for example, if someone slips on the ice and breaks a leg on your front steps, your insurance will pay.

Your insurance company will have standards as to how much insurance they will provide based on their assessed market value of your assets. You should ensure, though, that what will be paid out in insurance will at least cover any debt secured by that asset. For example, let's say you have a car on which you are making monthly payments. The insured value of the car is $6,000 but you still owe $7,500 on it. If the car is totaled, the financing company will immediately call the loan and you will have to dig up the excess $1,500 from somewhere to cover it.

When assessing whether your belongings are adequately covered by property and casualty insurance, make sure that you have considered any special collections you might own, such as stamps, art, hockey cards, or antiques. These types of assets are generally not covered under the standard policy and you may have to take out a special rider on them.

Health insurance

Health insurance is one area in which the majority of people are under-insured. It may be tempting to just assume that you will be healthy until you retire, but that is dangerous thinking. If your health fails, your ability to earn income may disappear, along with your plans for retirement.

As a small-business owner, health insurance is essential as you will not be able to rely on any employer- or government-funded health plans. There are two major coverages that you need to consider. The first is that you will not have your income any longer. As a small-business owner, you will have to hire someone to do the work that you once did or you may even have to close the doors, but either way, you will have to replace your former income. The second is that you may have ongoing medical and long-term care expenses in the future. For example, you may have to hire a private care nurse to attend to your medical needs.

There are many forms of health insurance. Some include coverage for drugs and dental expenses, some pay out a lump sum when you are diagnosed with a critical illness, and some provide ongoing payments for your lifetime. Discuss coverage with your financial adviser or insurance specialist to make sure that you will be able to continue to meet your personal and business financial goals in the event of serious illness.

Chapter Summary

➡ Before you jump into the role of business owner, it's important to first get your personal finances in shape.

➡ Reviewing your personal financial and retirement goals will help when you plan your business to ensure that all of your goals are in alignment.

➡ Getting your personal debt under control will help with your borrowing capacity in your business and will help you to manage your business debt more effectively.

➡ Having adequate insurance on all of your assets will help you to financially weather any catastrophic event.

Chapter

5

Setting Your Business Goals

What do you want from your business? Money? Status? Security? We look at the various goals of entrepreneurs and how to align your plan with your goals.

Introduction

We have spent considerable time so far discussing the personal side of your financial life because it forms a critical pillar to the success of your business. In this chapter, we begin to look at your business goals and how to set up your initial business plan.

By this point, you have considered what type of business you want to start and why you want to be an entrepreneur (Chapter 1). You have also thought about which opportunity will be best for you: Starting a business from scratch or buying an existing business (Chapter 3).

Now, you will need to start planning your business, including what your projected cash flows will be, when you will start to turn a profit, and how you will get out of your business when you're ready to do other things.

We will start by talking about money.

Chasing the Almighty Buck

Money may not be the only reason that you have decided to start up a small business. In fact, entrepreneurs tend to have an inborn need to create and build empires that reflect who they are and that can be passed on to future generations. But starting and managing a business is a risky venture and with risk comes the opportunity for reward.

Conventional wisdom says that you should sacrifice short-term monetary rewards for long-term gain. Many small-business owners not only do not think about getting a return on the money they have invested into their business, they don't even take a salary for the labor they invest. "I'll start taking a salary later when the business can afford it," is a refrain I frequently hear from small-business owners just starting out.

The danger of this thinking is that you may simply be subsidizing a business that cannot survive without you working and investing for free. The only successful business model is one that is able to pay all of its expenses as well as provide a return to its investors. Think about how long Microsoft would last if it couldn't pay its managers or pay dividends on its shares. Likewise, for your business to be successful, it will ultimately have to pay a manager, whether it's you or someone that you hire for the position.

Plan your remuneration right from the beginning. You know how much you will need from the business to pay your current expenses and you know how much you will have

to set aside every year to fund your retirement (see Chapter 4). This is the minimum remuneration that you will need to plan for. If your business will not have access to the external financing necessary to pay you as the manager, make sure that you know how long it will be before it is able to do so. For example, it is easier to forgo a salary if you know that, in six months, the business will start paying you one. This will also help with your own personal financial planning.

The bottom line is, even if money is not your primary motivation for starting your business, plan for profits and build your business model around profitability. Not only will it make your life more comfortable now, but it will increase the value of your business when it comes time to sell it or pass it on to the next generation (we'll talk more about exiting your business later in the chapter).

What Is the Purpose of Your Business?

The first step in planning your new business is to define what your business actually is. What will it provide to its customers? For example, if you want to open a hair salon, you must first define the range of services it will provide. Will it simply provide haircuts? Or will it be a full-service spa with high-end services like massage and facials?

The next planning step is to define your market. Who will your customers be? This will help you to target your marketing and promotions to be able to get at your potential customer base. This planning step will require some analysis. You need to make sure that the people you are targeting would really purchase your product or service. For example, if you have a car dealership that sells BMWs, you would more likely target wealthy business owners than penniless students. This may be a new concept for you if you have never run a business before and you may feel uncomfortable making generalizations about people based on their income or social stature. But you are simply trying to identify the group of consumers who are most likely to be interested in what you have to sell.

The third planning step is to identify where you want to be in your industry. If you are a massage therapist, do you want to be the least expensive? Be the most knowledgeable? Have the most flexible hours? This information will translate into your vision statement for your business: An all-encompassing statement about what your business stands for and what its mandate is. We will address developing a vision statement for your business in Part 2 of this book.

Once you have decided on the overall direction of your new business, it's time to start the detailed planning process.

The Business Plan

Every small-business owner is told to write a business plan before starting a small business. But what is a business plan really and who is it for?

Many small-business owners prepare a business plan solely because their bank demands that they do. They find a template online and fill in the blanks. Once the bank has reviewed it (or tucked it into a file without looking at it, as is often the case), the business owner never looks at it again and it collects dust on a shelf.

A business plan should, however, be a living, breathing, ever-changing document. It is the guidebook for your business to follow. It is to your business what the Constitution is to the United States: A set of guiding principles and the road map to get there. Remember, though, that the road map for your business will be constantly changing as you meet challenges in your business's operating environment and as you make changes to take advantage of new opportunities in the market. You will frequently review and update your business plan and compare your actual results to your plans.

The primary user of the business plan should be you, the owner. However, there will be many other potential users of your business plan, including:

- **Lenders.** They will want to make sure that they are lending money to a solid enterprise that has a probability of success.

- **Key employees.** When you hire a manager or other employee critical to the success of your business, you will want to make sure that he or she knows the business plan and will manage the business accordingly.

- **Investors.** Venture capitalists and other potential investors will want to ensure that their money will be well invested.

- **Customers.** There may be times where securing a large contract means providing background material on your business and the business plan is an important document in that context.

- **Potential merger partners or acquisition targets.** If you are proposing to merge with or buy another company, the owners of that company will want to make certain that your business is both financially and philosophically sound.

What Should Your Business Plan Include?

Your business plan should be detailed enough so that readers can understand what the business does and how it will go about doing it, but not too long or detailed that they will get lost in the minutia.

There are as many opinions on what should be included in a business plan as there are advisers, but Sample 5 is an example of critical information that should be included. Note also that you may alter your basic business plan depending on the reader. For example, a bank may be interested in very different information than a key employee. Be prepared to tailor your plan to different groups of readers.

At first, the sheer volume of the information required for this document may overwhelm you, but take it one piece at a time. All of this information should be thought about and planned out before you open your doors. It may take several months for you to gather and plan the information. The more upfront planning you do, however, the more probability of success you will have.

The Monthly Management Operating Plan

Once you have mapped out the overall direction and strategy that your business will take in your business plan, it's time to start looking at how you will manage the ongoing operations. How will you know if your revenues are on track? Will you have enough money next month to pay your suppliers? All these questions are answered in the monthly management operating plan (or the MMOP). The MMOP allows you to regularly monitor the operations of your business. It will tell you instantly if you are on track with your profit projections or if your liquidity is less than planned. Your MMOP should contain the following information:

- A monthly budget showing actual-versus-planned figures

- A monthly cash flow statement showing actual-versus-planned figures

- Ratio analysis, including turnover and capital ratios

- An analysis of all actual key performance indicators compared to the plan

- A synopsis of the external and internal business environment and how it has affected the business

- A thorough analysis of employee productivity

- A summary of promotional efforts and their measurable impact on results

Your monthly management operating plan should give you an analysis at a glance. In the beginning when you are the only employee in the business, you will be pulling this information yourself from your bookkeeping system, updating the plan, and then reviewing the results. As you grow, you will simply be reviewing the results and others will be

SAMPLE 5
BUSINESS PLAN OUTLINE

BUSINESS PLAN OUTLINE

I. EXECUTIVE SUMMARY
1. Overall purpose of the business
2. The competition and the business's place in the industry
3. The market
4. Growth strategy
5. Profitability and projections
6. Human resources
7. Financing structure and requirements

II. EXTERNAL ENVIRONMENT AND INDUSTRY ANALYSIS
1. Geographical operating environment and constraints
2. The industry
3. Product or service analysis
4. Development and operating strategy

III. THE MARKET
1. Market size in the geographical operating environment
2. Competitive analysis of market servicing
3. Customer group profile
4. Market share growth strategy

IV. OPERATIONAL MANAGEMENT
1. Cash flow projections: 12 months and 5 years
2. Break-even and capacity analysis
3. Cost structure of business
4. Profitability potential and timing
5. Operating location and warehousing
6. Operating cycle
7. Life cycle timing

V. MARKETING AND PROMOTION
1. Competitive strategy
2. Sales strategies and outlets
3. Pricing analysis
4. Advertising strategy
5. Product distribution or service provision
6. Servicing

VI. GROWTH STRATEGY
1. Overall growth strategy
2. Financing plan
3. Growth limitations and constraints
4. External and internal challenges and obstacles
5. New product or service development and introduction
6. Exit and harvest strategies

VII. HUMAN RESOURCES
1. Organizational structure
2. Key employee profiles
3. Ownership and investment structure
4. Remuneration and performance evaluation
5. Governance
6. External advisory team

VIII. FINANCING REQUIREMENTS
1. Amount and use of required funds
2. Current debt/equity structure
3. Proposed return on funds

IX. HISTORICAL FINANCIAL INFORMATION (when available)
1. Balance sheet
2. Income statement
3. Statement of cash flows
4. Ratio analysis

doing the mechanical gathering. For a more detailed discussion of the MMOP and how to calculate ratios and develop key performance indicators, please refer to the second book in the *Numbers 101 for Small Business* series, *Financial Management 101*.

Your Exit Strategy

It may seem strange to talk about getting out of your business before you've even gotten into it, but you should plan your leave-taking right from the beginning. The main reason for this is that you never know when you will be leaving. Even if you plan on running your business literally until you drop, that day may come sooner than you're expecting and your heirs will be left with the task of harvesting the value that you have built up in your business. Another reason for planning your leave is to make sure that your business is always working in concert with your retirement goals. If you expect to make a $100,000 gain on the sale of your business to help fund your retirement, you need to plan the growth that will be required for that gain right from the beginning. Your exit strategy will be included as a part of your business plan and may change over time as the external environment and your business goals change.

Chapter Summary

➥ A successful business model is able to pay all the expenses of the business and a return to the investors, so planning for your own remuneration and profit is important.

➥ Your business planning should start with your overall vision for the business, whom it ill serve, and how it will operate.

➥ Your business plan is a living, breathing, ever-changing document that guides your business operations and growth adhering to its underlying principles.

➥ The monthly management operating plan compares your actual operating results to your plans to make sure that you're on track.

Putting Your Money Where Your Business Plan Is

A look at capitalizing your business. How much money will you need? Where will it come from? How expensive is it going to be?

Introduction

A business can only grow as fast as its capital allows. Capital can come from three sources, either solely, or a combination of the three:

- Your own resources

- Resources of an external investor

- Revenue generated from your business

Eventually, internally generated revenue will provide the operating capital for the business. Profits will be plowed back in to the business to allow it to keep a war chest or savings for the bad times or to finance further growth and expansion. In the beginning, however, you will have to rely on your own resources or those of an external investor.

It's important that, as part of your business plan, you identify and quantify your financing needs. You will need cash for some or all of these reasons:

- **Start-up costs.** Your initial investment into the business might include inventory, equipment purchases, rental deposits, and legal and accounting fees.

- **Shortfalls of revenues over expenses.** You will still need to pay your suppliers and pay the fixed costs of running the business even before you become profitable.

- **War chest.** This is simply a fund of money (or short-term investments) set aside for a rainy day or for taking advantage of sudden opportunities.

- **Capital equipment replacement.** Eventually, your equipment will break down or become obsolete and you will have to re-invest in new equipment.
- **Growth.** Expansion of your current operations may mean additional costs related to advertising, payroll, warehousing, or product research and development. You will likely incur these costs before you generate the revenues as a result of the expansion.

Let's have a look at how to project your need for capital.

Projecting Your Funding Needs

The process of raising cash is not limited to starting up your business. You will have ongoing need for capital in all stages of your business. Financing needs to be an integrated part of your ongoing operational and strategic management.

In the start-up phase, however, you have two initial concerns:

1. Paying for the start-up costs
2. Providing liquidity to the business until the revenues can sustain it

Paying for the start-up costs

When outlining your necessary start-up costs, take your time and ensure that you are capturing all the costs that there are. You may forget seemingly insignificant things that can add up to you shelling out several more thousand dollars upfront than you expected. Typical start-up costs include the following:

- **Purchase of initial inventory.** This will clearly be more important for a retail operation or manufacturer.

CASE STUDY

Craig had now met with his partner, Gordon, for the visioning session and had prepared the initial business plan for Earth-Power. Both partners were excited about the new venture and had created a list of potential investors and lenders. They had determined that they needed at least $195,000 to get started, which would pay for their start-up expenses as well as the first nine months of operations, when their projected expenses would be more than their revenues.

The partners decided to meet with their bankers first to find out the bank's position on funding their venture. Gordon also wanted the two to meet with a private investor who provided investment funds to new companies that provide alternative energy solutions.

Before meeting with potential lenders, Craig and Gordon met with Vivian again to work on their presentation. They knew that they would only have one opportunity to present themselves and their new company to lenders. They needed to think about and have answers to the questions that lenders would ask them. They also needed to have well-thought out cash flow projections based on conservative estimates of the business's growth and revenue patterns.

Once the partners worked out all the bugs in their presentation, they approached their respective banks to see if they could get debt financing. Craig's bank declined to offer financing as the venture was too new and did not have a financial track record. Gordon's bank, however, was willing to lend them $125,000 at 7 percent in exchange for a general security agreement, which meant that the bank was using the assets of the business as collateral for the loan. Craig and Gordon then approached the private investor who offered to put up the final $70,000 in exchange for a 10 percent ownership stake in the company. The partners discussed the offer extensively before finally deciding that giving away a small piece of the company was a fair price to pay for the needed financing.

They were finally ready to prepare for the start up of their new business.

- **Capital equipment.** Not only will you have to buy any equipment that you need to make the product or provide the service, but you may need peripheral equipment like vehicles, computers, and office furniture.
- **Rental deposits.** You may have to pay a deposit on your rented location or on any rented office equipment.
- **Supplies.** Although items like pens, paper, and staplers don't seem significant, the initial cost of stocking your office can be high.
- **Insurance premiums.** Although you may pay monthly premiums in the future for liability or business insurance, your carrier may require that you pay the first year upfront.
- **Professional fees.** You may incur legal and accounting fees to set up your business and also to retain advice on planning and strategizing.
- **Renovation costs.** You may need to design and build or renovate your interior office or store space. Costs can include designing, carpentry, painting, carpet, sound systems, and a host of other expenses.
- **Delay costs.** This is an expense that smart entrepreneurs factor into their calculations. If you can't open your doors on time because the space isn't ready or the product isn't available, you will still be incurring all of the operational costs of running the business without the revenues that you had planned.

Once you have outlined and valued all your projected start-up costs, build in a cushion, anywhere from 5 percent to 10 percent of your total costs, to give you some breathing room in case of cost overruns.

Providing liquidity to the business

The second requirement for cash will come from the cash flow projections you have prepared as part of your business plan. Whenever your projected cash balance falls below zero, you have a shortfall that you will have to finance. For example, if you are expecting cash shortfalls in the first three months of $5,000, $3,200, and $1,450 respectively before you start generating net cash surpluses, you will need to find $9,650 in funding for the shortfalls. Once again, build in a cushion in case your shortfalls exceed those planned.

Let's have a closer look at putting together your cash flow projection. Sample 6 is an example of a cash flow projection that has been reproduced from the second book in the *Numbers 101 for Small Business* series, *Financial Management 101*. There are several important things to note as you are preparing your own cash flow projection:

1. Keep in mind the difference between cash flows and revenues and expenses. Cash flow refers to the actual inflows and outflows of cash, whereas revenues and expenses (as reported on the income statement) can reflect items where the cash transaction hasn't yet occurred. For example, if you sell an item today but your customer won't pay you for 30 days, this will show up on an income statement as a revenue item, but would not show up in a cash flow report because you haven't received the money yet. The cash flow projection deals only with actual inflows and outflows of money. Its purpose is to make sure that you don't run out of money.

2. The "Cash receipts" line reflects your estimate of the actual receipt of accounts receivable, not your sales projections. For example, you may collect

Sample 6
CASH FLOW PROJECTION

Small Company Inc.
Cash flow report
January – December 2009

	Jan	Feb	Mar	Apr	May	Jun	Jul	Aug	Sep	Oct	Nov	Dec	Total
Cash receipts	3,725	4,612	4,109	3,289	5,085	5,139	4,103	3,578	3,945	4,210	6,412	5,303	53,510
Cost of goods sold	1,895	2,416	1,989	1,675	2,756	2,708	1,965	1,792	2,006	2,165	3,260	2,585	27,212
Advertising	50	50	50	50	50	50	103	50	50	50	50	50	653
Bank charges	7	7	7	7	7	7	7	7	7	7	7	17	94
Office expenses	61	68	66	72	69	65	73	57	53	65	76	71	796
Professional fees	-	-	-	412	-	-	-	-	-	-	-	-	412
Supplies	39	31	42	19	65	58	17	39	42	58	63	51	524
Telephone and utilities	87	89	79	96	85	89	97	89	71	69	59	76	986
Vehicle expenses	39	47	32	45	49	51	34	31	32	41	39	38	478
Wages	306	310	285	296	314	312	342	284	292	325	312	295	3,673
Purchase of capital equipment	-	-	-	1,953	-	475	-	-	-	710	-	-	3,138
Net cash inflow (outflow)	1,241	1,594	1,559	(1,336)	1,690	1,324	1,465	1,229	1,392	720	2,546	2,120	15,544
Opening cash	1,259	2,500	4,094	5,653	4,317	6,007	7,331	8,796	10,025	11,417	12,137	14,683	
Closing cash	2,500	4,094	5,653	4,317	6,007	7,331	8,796	10,025	11,417	12,137	14,683	16,803	

only 15 percent of your revenues in the month of sale, 63 percent the following month, 18 percent in two months, and 4 percent in three months. Sample 7 is an example of what that might look like.

Notice that although you are reporting $1,250 in sales for the month of January, your cash flow report would only show cash receipts of $187.50. Make sure when you are preparing your cash flow projection that you take into consideration the average length of time it will take to collect your receivables.

3. All cash receipts and cash payments appear on the cash flow projection, regardless of their source. In the example, there is a line for the purchase of capital equipment. This item would not be recorded on the income statement (it is a balance sheet item) but it is a payment of cash. Any projected purchases such as equipment and inventory should be included in your projection. The same would be true of proceeds from a new loan. If the bank lends you $25,000, it would show as a receipt of cash on the cash flow report.

4. If the closing cash balance on the cash flow projection falls below zero at the end of any month, you will have to consider how to finance the shortfall. It is okay to have a net cash outflow in any particular month (as in the month of April in the example) as long as there is a cumulative cash surplus going into the month. This would roughly translate to a positive projected balance in the business bank account, which would be able to absorb any shortfall up to that balance. It is only when the cumulative balance drops below zero (i.e., you have no money in the bank account) that you have to have other financing in place.

To brush up on bookkeeping basics, take a look at *Bookkeepers' Boot Camp,* the first book in the *Numbers 101 for Small Business* series.

Sources of Funding

Because funding in the start-up period is not likely to come from net profits right away, you must look to either your own resources or those of other lenders or investors.

Your own resources could include:

- Savings
- Personal loan or line of credit
- Re-mortgage of your house
- Credit cards
- Borrowings from family or friends

Some of these sources are preferable to others. We will discuss these in more detail in the next chapter.

Other lender or investor funds could include:

- Business bank loans
- Business lines of credit
- Business credit cards
- Private loans
- Leaseback agreements
- Business property mortgages
- Stock sales (in the case of corporations)
- Venture capitalists
- Joint venture partnerships

As with personal borrowing, some types of business borrowings are preferable to others and will be discussed in the following two chapters. Some of these sources of funding represent equity, or ownership, stakes in the business, while others represent debt to outside parties. The type of borrowing may have an effect on the debt to equity ratio of the business, which may impact the ability of the business to borrow further funds.

SAMPLE 7
CASH INFLOWS

	Jan	Feb	Mar	Apr	May
Revenue	1,250.00	1,095.00	2,470.00	1,750.00	975.00
Collected:					
Current (15%)	187.50	164.25	370.50	262.50	146.25
Next month (63%)		787.50	689.85	1,556.10	1,102.50
2 months (18%)			225.00	197.10	444.60
3 months (4%)				50.00	43.80
Total Cash Inflow	**187.50**	**951.75**	**1,285.35**	**2,065.70**	**1,737.15**

A Bank's Perspective

Let's have a look at financing from the bank's perspective. This will be a useful viewpoint to keep in mind as you are preparing to see your banker.

You are the bank manager at a small regional bank. Tony has called you this morning and has set up an appointment to see you at two o'clock this afternoon. Tony and his wife have been personal banking clients at your bank for over ten years. Tony has been a mechanic at the local car dealership for as long as you have known him. Today on the telephone, he has told you briefly about his plan to start his own auto repair shop. He is coming to you today to discuss financing the new business. As a bank manager entrusted with the safety of the bank's money, what are the most important considerations you will have when deciding whether Tony gets the funding? Clearly, you will be concerned with his ability to make the loan payments. In order to make the loan payments, Tony will have to make enough money in his new business to cover them off. He will be quitting his job to start the business and his wife stays at home with the household and children, so his only source of income will be the new business.

The second thing that you will consider is how to protect the bank's interests if the business is not as successful as planned and Tony defaults on the payments. The bank will want to be able to use some of Tony's other assets to settle the outstanding debt so that the bank is not out of pocket for the remaining balance of the loan.

In order to get comfort on both of those issues, there are a number of things that you will be looking for Tony to be able to demonstrate to you when he comes to see you this afternoon:

- **Is the business built on a solid plan?** How much "homework" has Tony done to prove that this is a viable business venture?

- **Does he have enough entrepreneurial skills to build and manage a business?** Tony has indicated that he will be responsible for the ongoing management of the operation, so you will need some idea as to whether he has any training or ability in finance, bookkeeping, operational management, strategic planning, and human resource management.

- **Is the business built on a model that will have sufficient cash flow to pay its creditors, including your bank?** As a bank manager, you have to be concerned not only with your bank's exposure to Tony's risk of failure, but the exposure of other lenders. For example, if Tony is able to make your bank's loan payments but defaults on the mortgage on the repair shop, the mortgage lender can foreclose on the property, leaving Tony without a business or source of income.
- **Does Tony have enough assets to satisfy the outstanding amount of the** loan if he defaults on the payments? The last thing that you want is to have Tony not make his payments and the bank having to seize assets, but you certainly want to have that option open to you as a last resort.

These are the major concerns of any lender. Keep these in mind when you prepare your business plan and when you see your banker. Make sure that you have the answers to the questions that he or she is most likely to ask. For more information on getting a loan from a bank, check out *Financial Management 101*, the second book in the *Numbers 101 for Small Business* series.

Chapter Summary

➡ During the start-up phase, your business will most likely need financing from your own personal resources or from an outside lender.

➡ You will need to finance your start-up expenses and any shortfall in revenues over expenses until your business begins to turn a profit.

➡ External financing can come from one or more of a number of sources, including banks, venture capitalists, investors, and private lenders.

➡ Prepare answers ahead of time to address the most likely questions that your banker (or other lenders) will ask you when you seek financing.

Chapter
7

Debt Financing

Debt is a common source of funding a business. In this chapter we examine the pros and cons of borrowing.

Introduction

Once you have determined the dollar amount of capital that you need to fund the start-up phase of your business, it's time to start evaluating the potential sources of financing. In this chapter, we will look at debt financing. In the next, we will examine sources of equity financing.

Debt financing can take many forms but it basically means that a lender has loaned you funds that you are obligated to repay in the future. Debt financing doesn't involve an ownership stake in the business, but simply a promise to pay. That promise can take several forms, depending on the financing tool and the guarantees involved.

When considering debt financing, *who* you are borrowing from is just as important as *what*

you are borrowing. An experienced lender, such as a bank or a venture capitalist, can assist with advice as well as money, whereas borrowing from friends or relatives can often cause more headaches than it solves if they choose to interfere in business affairs.

Another important consideration is the term of financing. You may need to borrow capital to pay for the land and building upon which you operate. These are long-term assets and should be backed with long-term financing. Think of what would happen if you took out a two-year term loan on the property and couldn't refinance at the end of two years. Make sure that the term of the financing matches the term of the underlying assets.

Let's look at some of the more common forms of debt financing and their characteristics.

Your Own Resources

This is the first place you should start for many reasons. First, using your own funds is the least risky proposition from an asset seizure point of view. You (the lender or investor) are not likely to foreclose on you (the borrower). Second, external lenders will want to see that you have funds at risk, that is to say that you believe enough in your venture to put your own hard-earned cash into it. If you want the external lenders to risk their capital, you should have something at stake as well.

You may have to save for a considerable amount of time to start your own business. Other financing may be scarce in the beginning and the more of your own savings you have, the better the likelihood of financial stability and growth.

It is important to remember, however, that, just as you wouldn't invest all of your life's savings in a single stock, you shouldn't put all of your eggs in the same basket by dumping it all into your business. Make sure that you have a number of savings vehicles for the future.

Credit Cards

Just as in your personal financial life, credit cards can be a dangerous source of business financing. Many entrepreneurs have run up their cards to the limit to generate the start-up capital needed for their business. This generally happens when a small-business owner doesn't qualify for bank financing.

The problems with credit cards are many. First, the interest rate tends to be exorbitant. Credit card rates do not tend to move with changes in market interest rates, so even when other rates are low, credit card rates can be upwards of 20 percent per annum. Second, if you do not qualify for bank financing in the first place, running up a high balance on your credit cards will more than likely guarantee that the banks will look even more unfavorably on you in the future.

It may be tempting to be overly optimistic and think that you will be able to pay down the credit cards quickly but you must remember that there are many uncontrollable variables in starting a business that may require more capital than you expected.

Bottom line: Try to avoid credit cards as much as possible. If you do use them for starting up your business, make sure that you pay them off as quickly as possible. Also, make sure that you at least pay the minimum amounts required and pay them on time; late credit card payments show up on your credit rating.

Suppliers

Suppliers are often a much-overlooked source of financing for a new business. Most suppliers offer credit terms on purchases, ranging anywhere from 15 to 90 days on average. If you take advantage of your suppliers' credit terms, make sure that payments are made on time. Suppliers can charge a late payment penalty that can be higher than credit card rates.

Some suppliers offer an early payment discount that can equate to a very large savings. For example, if a supplier offers 2/10 net 30 terms, this means that you get an early payment discount of 2 percent if the bill is paid in 10 days; otherwise it's due in 30 days. If, for example, your purchase was for $1,000, you would only have to pay $980 if you pay within 10 days. Another way to look at it is to say that 2 percent will buy you an extra 20 days of credit. But how much does that credit really cost?

By not taking the discount, you are borrowing $980 for an extra 20 days and paying $20 for that privilege ($1,000 minus $980). The interest rate for the period is 2.04 percent ($20 ÷ $980 = 2.04%).

There are 18.25 20-day periods in the year (365 ÷ 20). The effective annual rate (EAR) is calculated as:

$$EAR = (1+0.0204)^{18.25} - 1 = 44.6\%$$

You are essentially paying an interest rate of 44.6 percent to borrow the funds for an extra 20 days. That's pretty expensive credit! Another way to look at it is to say that you are making 44.6 percent on your money by taking the discount.

On the other end of the spectrum, many suppliers charge interest on overdue accounts. A common term of sale is 2 percent interest per month for each month overdue. What is the true cost of taking advantage of this form of financing? At first glance, it would appear to be 24 percent annually (2 percent X 12 months), but it is actually higher than that, due to the negative pull of compounding. The effective annual rate is actually:

$$EAR = (1+0.02)^{12} - 1 = 26.82\% \text{ annually}$$

It would therefore cost you 26.82 percent to use this source of financing beyond 30 days. That is higher than bank financing and even higher than most credit cards. You must weigh this cost against the short-term cash flow benefit of using this source of financing.

Another issue to think about when deciding if you will pay later than stipulated by the supplier is the impact on your credit rating with that supplier. Getting an extra 20 days of credit might not be worth having the supplier put you on a cash-only basis in the future because you don't pay on time.

Bottom line: Use your suppliers' credit terms but beware the cost (in terms of dollars and credit history) of not paying them on time.

Friends and Family

Your friends and family may have many different reasons for wanting to lend money to your new business. They may want to help you out by giving you that little boost when you're first starting out. They may be shrewd investors, knowing that you'll walk barefoot over broken glass to pay them back.

As we have discussed previously, it may be very difficult for you to attract outside capital before you have established a track record. Friends and family may be your only option for a while. Before you borrow from people you know, take the following into consideration:

- Make certain that your understanding of the arrangement is the same as that of the lender and that you have thoroughly discussed all aspects of the proposed loan.

- Fully document the loan just as the bank would if the bank were lending to you. Spell out the term, interest rate, repayment terms, and any security that may be pledged against the loan. Have both parties sign a copy of the loan agreement.

- Treat the loan as a business arrangement. Be sure that you make repayments on time and that you don't let things "slide" because it's someone you know.

- Make sure that the loan is handled properly from a tax perspective. In many jurisdictions, you will not be able to deduct the interest that you pay on the loan for tax purposes if the lender does not claim the interest income. This could significantly raise your effective cost of borrowing. Discuss the proposed loan with your accountant before signing.

Bottom line: Proceed with caution when borrowing from friends and family and make sure that the arrangement is well documented and formalized.

Banks

Banks can assist you with many different types of financing and will most likely be one of the cornerstones of your business. Banks can provide:

- Lines of credit
- Unsecured loans
- Receivables financing
- Loans secured by property or equipment
- Loans secured by the owner's personal guarantee (and assets)
- Mortgage financing

As discussed in the previous chapter, make sure that you have thoroughly thought through your financing needs before you see your banker, so that you can be clear about what type of financing you are seeking.

Banks will be very interested in what types of assets (personal and business) you have with which they can secure the loan, especially when you are just starting out and do not yet have a financial history. Loans that are secured with assets will generally be at a lower interest rate than unsecured loans. However, if you default on a secured loan, you will risk losing the asset that backs the loan. If that asset is your residence, you risk homelessness. Always make sure that you understand what assets you are risking when signing a bank loan.

Banks may also have other stipulations when lending to your small business, including required liquidity ratios and restrictions on other debt. If your business fails to meet these requirements at any time over the course of the loan (called "going offside"), the bank can call the loan and you may find yourself scrambling for another quick source of funds.

Table 1 provides a summary of financial ratios. For a more detailed discussion of ratios, please refer to *Financial Management 101*, the second book in the *Numbers 101 for Small Business* series.

Bottom line: Bank financing may be difficult to get in the start-up period and may have many restrictions attached to it. However, it is a lower cost financing solution that forms the basis of most small business funding.

Leasing Companies

Leasing companies specialize in financing manufacturing or office equipment. You may find that the company that you purchase the equipment from has its own leasing arm and can handle the entire transaction for you.

Equipment leases are always secured by the equipment being leased, so if you fall behind on your payments, you risk losing the equipment. On the other hand, the interest rates tend to be low on this type of finance both because of its secured nature and also because the leasing company may be using the lease as a purchase incentive.

It can sometimes be difficult to ascertain the effective interest rate on a lease so always make sure you thoroughly read the documents and discuss any questions with your accountant. Knowing, for example, that you will pay $450 per month for 60 months tells you nothing about the rate of interest you are paying. Repairs and maintenance is another area that you need to be clear on. Who is responsible if the equipment breaks down during the term of the lease: you or the leasing company? Also, make sure that you understand what happens at the end of the term. Some leases simply turn the ownership over to you at that point. Others require a buyout and you will need to figure that into your calculations.

Bottom line: Leasing can be a great way to finance equipment purchases, but it's important to make sure that you understand exactly what you're paying.

TABLE 1
A QUICK REFERENCE TO RATIOS

Solvency or liquidity ratios

1. Current ratio = Current assets ÷ Current liabilities

Am I going to be able to pay my short-term debts?

2. Total debt ratio = Total debt ÷ Total assets

How much leverage do I have?

Asset and debt management ratios

3. Inventory turnover = COGS ÷ Inventory

How long before I sell my product?

4. Receivables turnover = Sales ÷ Accounts receivable

How long before I get paid for what I sell?

5. Payables turnover = COGS ÷ Accounts payable

How quickly do I pay my suppliers?

6. Times interest earned = EBIT ÷ Interest expense

Do I have enough income to pay the interest on my debt?

Profitability ratios

7. Profit margin = Net income ÷ Sales

How efficiently am I managing my expenses?

8. Return on assets = Net profit ÷ Total assets

How well am I using my assets to generate profit?

9. Return on investment = Normalized net income ÷ money invested

What kind of return am I getting on the money I've put into the business?

Private Lenders

Like banks, private lending is used in many different applications. The most common, however, is borrowing from a private lender because you have been turned down for other types of financing. Because of the increased risk to the lender (who would definitely know that the bank wouldn't deal with you), the interest rates charged in these types of situations tend to be high.

There are private lenders, sometimes referred to as "angel investors," who enjoy the financial risk and the accompanying thrill of helping a new business to get off the ground. These lenders can be difficult to find, but speak with your lawyer, accountant, or financial planner about whether they have the appropriate contacts.

The biggest danger with using a private lender is hidden fees. In some cases there are none, but make sure that you read through the entire agreement (and it's generally a good idea to let your lawyer review the document as well) before you sign anything. You should understand all aspects of the loan, including interest rate, repayment terms, initial or renewal fees, assets secured, and fees charged for missed or bounced payments.

Bottom line: Private lenders may be your source of last resort but make sure you understand the whole picture.

Chapter Summary

➡ Debt financing involves borrowing funds and repaying them over time, with interest, to the lender.

➡ Loans that are secured with equipment, real estate, or other assets tend to have lower interest rates than unsecured loans.

➡ You should look to your own savings first as your best source of funds.

➡ When borrowing from outside sources, make sure you understand the whole agreement before signing.

Chapter

8

Equity Financing

Another source of funds is through the sale of ownership in the business. We look at the major considerations in this chapter.

Introduction

Another potential source of financing is equity financing. Equity financing differs from debt financing in a few key ways. It usually involves a longer term investment than debt financing. As the recipient of the funds, you will pay a return to the investor, usually in the form of dividends. You generally do not pay back the original investment unless the investor wants to "cash out."

Equity financing also generally involves two other features: Ownership share and profit participation. When an investor takes an equity stake in your business, he or she is buying a slice of the pie. You are transferring some of the risks and rewards of ownership of your business over to the investor. Because the risk

to the investor is greater than in a loan situation, the investor will expect a higher return in the form of dividends. Dividends may be a fixed payment (similar to a loan's interest rate) or may be a percentage of the after-tax net profits of the business, depending on the type of investment. We will look at the common types of equity investments in more detail later in the chapter.

Finding people willing to invest in your start-up business for the long term may be quite difficult. Your business does not yet have an established financial track record and the risks may outstrip the appetites of many potential investors. Start-up businesses tend to have more debt financing in the beginning stages and then slowly convert towards more equity financing as the business reaches the maturity stage of its life cycle.

Let's take a look at the characteristics of some of the more common types of equity investments.

Common Shares

Common shareholders are the owners of a corporation. For example, if you own 50 percent of the common shares of a corporation, you own 50 percent of the business. The dividends paid to the common shareholders are set by the board of directors and are equal in proportion to the shareholdings. In a small incorporated corporation, you are most likely the president and you would, therefore, decide what dividends are to be paid out to the common shareholders (a group of which you are likely a member as well).

Common shareholders also have voting rights in the corporation. If you have sold, for example, 55 percent of the common shares of your corporation, those shares can control the vote. You may find yourself without any way to influence the decision making in your own business. Even if the minority shareholders own less than 50 percent, they can still meddle in the affairs of the business and slow down its operations or growth.

When a corporation winds up, it pays its liabilities from its assets. Whatever is left (if anything) goes to the common shareholders. If that company is insolvent (one of the main reasons for wind up), the investors may not be able to recover their original investment.

Because dividend payments are out of the control of the investors and because of the risk of loss of the original investment, it is unlikely that you will be able to attract common shareholders in your start-up business; however, you may wish to pursue this type of financing as you grow.

Preferred Shares

Preferred share arrangements come in all colors and stripes. Although preferred shares still represent an ownership stake in the corporation, they frequently are stripped of their voting and profit participation rights. In exchange for giving up those rights, preferred shareholders receive a higher ranking on the list of payouts when the company winds up. In other words, preferred shareholders will be paid before common shareholders.

Another common feature of preferred shares is a fixed dividend rate. Instead of having to wait and see if there's any profit to distribute, preferred shares may be paid, for example, a 6 percent fixed dividend. This dividend payment would also rank higher than any potential dividend payments to the common shareholders. As the value of the dividend is fixed, when interest rates fall in the market place, these shares become more valuable and can be sold for a gain above what was originally invested.

Partnership

A partnership is a non-incorporated company owned by two or more individuals or corporations. Each partner would have an equity statement showing his or her original investment, the accumulated net income accruing to each partner, the draws that have been taken against that income, and the ending equity balance. Table 2 is an example of an equity statement for a 50/50 partnership.

Note how each partner has contributed the same amount of capital and that the income over the years has been split 50/50 in accordance with the partnership percentages. Joe and Melissa may choose to withdraw this fund of capital at a different rate, depending on the need for money and tax considerations. So, it is quite possible that partners may have different net equity positions at any point in time.

When the partnership winds up, the partners will split whatever is left over after the liabilities are satisfied with the assets based on their equity positions. It is hoped that they will be able to receive the dollar amount of

TABLE 2
EQUITY STATEMENT FOR A 50/50 PARTNERSHIP

	Joe	Melissa	Total
Original investment	$43,000	$43,000	$86,000
Cumulative profit	129,000	129,000	258,000
Current year profit	30,410	30,410	60,820
Draws	(157,000)	(62,530)	219,530
Net equity	$45,410	$139,880	$185,290

their net equity positions, but, for example, if there was only $71,050 left to distribute back to the partners, Joe would get $17,413 (45,410/185,290 x 71,050) and Melissa would get $53,637 (139,880/185,290 x 71,050).

You may choose to bring partners on board to finance your start-up or expansion. Keep in mind that partners will most likely want to have a say in the business's operations. Make sure that the partnership agreement has had every facet spelled out in detail, including how decisions are made. Each partner's lawyer should review the document before signing to make sure that nothing has been overlooked.

It's very tempting on start-up to partner with someone. You both have vision for the company and have a very rosy outlook on its chances. It is at this point that a partnership agreement should be signed. Down the road, if there are disagreements, the partnership agreement should spell out how the impasse is handled. Signed agreements make good partners!

Joint Ventures

A joint venture in its simplest sense is a short-term partnership. Let's say that you own a business that is a wholesaler of sporting goods. That means that you purchase the goods from the manufacturer and sell to retail stores. You have run across an unusual situation that can be very profitable. One of the manufacturers that you deal with has a surplus of 75,000 trail bikes. The manufacturer is willing to sell the whole lot to you for $57 a piece, for a total of $4,275,000. You are certain that you can sell these to retailers in a short period of time and make a substantial profit. The only problem is that you don't have over four million dollars lying around. You would then look for a joint venture partner: someone who is willing to put up the money in order to split the profits on the sale.

Joint ventures are a win-win situation. They differ from partnerships in that they relate to very specific activities. Each joint venturer, whether it's an individual or a company, may have other business operations on his or her own.

Forming a joint venture can be a great way of taking advantage of opportunities that cross your path as you grow your business, but, like every other type of joint ownership arrangement, it's important to map out everything in a signed agreement before starting the project.

Venture Capitalists

Venture capitalists are a unique breed. They seek out businesses that they feel have tremendous opportunities for growth and profit. Then they invest funds in these businesses and harvest a piece of the profit at a later date. There are several considerations for you to look at when deciding whether to approach a venture capitalist for financing:

- Venture capitalists usually only fund existing businesses that have a track record of stability and a future potential of large profits.

- Venture capitalists are very hands on. Most have extensive business or management experience and want to help to drive the direction of the company. This can be very beneficial if you are deficient in these skills, but can also cause friction.

- Venture capitalists are interested only in increasing the worth of their equity stake. To that end, they will position the company towards going public or selling out to a larger company. This is how they will get their reward in the end. You may find yourself ending up with very little say in the company.

- Venture capitalists can find new markets and new acquisition targets for your company that you may not have thought of or had access to.

Before you seek out a venture capitalist, make sure that your goals for your business will align with the goals of the investor. If the venture capitalist makes money, you make money. You get to go along for the ride. You just may not be in the driver's seat.

Chapter Summary

➡ Equity financing is more permanent than debt financing and involves giving up an ownership stake in your business in exchange for capital.

➡ Common and preferred shares represent the ownership of a corporation with different risks and rewards.

➡ Partnerships are long-term pairings of individuals or corporations for business purposes, while joint ventures are pairings for specific and finite projects.

➡ Venture capitalists invest in businesses with great profit and growth potential in exchange for operational control.

Chapter
9

Risky Business:
How to Assess Business Risk

Do you really know what's at stake in your business? We look at business risk, from the chance of losing your home to collection issues.

Introduction

No one likes to contemplate risk. If you're a small-business owner, you certainly don't want to think about your business as being risky. But entrepreneurs are notorious for two things: overestimating profit potential and underestimating risk.

Risk lurks in every situation where you are obligated to perform certain things even when the situation or business climate changes. The risk to you is that the business will lose assets and profit. It is certainly true that along with risk comes the potential for reward, which is one of the main reasons for

starting your business in the first place. It is critical, though, to make sure that you have a handle on your exposure to the risks in your business, both those that exist naturally and those that exist because of how the business is being managed.

Let's have a look at some common risks that you may be exposed to in your business and how to minimize them.

Secured Loans

In Chapter 7, we discussed how having your loan secured with business assets (be they equipment, vehicles, or real estate) would generally mean a lower interest rate than with an unsecured loan. The other side of that coin, however, is that if you default on the loan payments, the lender has a right to repossess (repo) the assets that secure the loan. For example, if you have purchased $100,000 worth of manufacturing equipment with bank financing but have not achieved the level of planned profitability and therefore have fallen behind on loan payments, the bank may take the equipment away and sell it to try to recoup the outstanding amount on the loan. It would be impossible for you to operate without equipment and you may be hard pressed to find anyone else willing to lend to you with your default history.

Minimize the risk of losing your secured assets by carefully monitoring your cash flows and ensuring that you make all payments on time and meet all terms of the loan.

Personal Guarantees

A lender may require the personal guarantee of the business owner when there are not enough business assets to secure the financing. A personal guarantee means that if the business defaults on its obligations, you will be on the hook for the repayment whether or not the business is a separate legal entity.

A lender may go further than a general personal guarantee and may secure the business loan directly with personal assets, including the equity in your home, vehicles, and investment portfolios. The lender may take these assets from you to satisfy the terms of the business loan if the repayment terms are not met. Having personal assets secured may also make it difficult for you to seek personal financing such as investment loans or house mortgages.

Minimize this risk by seeking the lowest rate financing that does not require personal guarantees. If it is impossible to avoid a personal guarantee, revisit the issue with your lender on a regular basis to see if the guarantee can be waived after some history of prompt payment.

Fixed Price Agreements

Fixed price agreements can protect your business from inflation and price changes if used properly but can dramatically increase your risk if handled improperly.

Let's look at an example. You own a transportation company and have negotiated an agreement with a large poultry farm to ship chickens across the country in the coming year at a set price per mile. After the agreement has been signed, the government institutes a new "road tax" that will charge vehicle owners six cents per mile driven to help pay for roads and policing. The cost of providing the transportation service to your customer has increased dramatically, but, because you signed a fixed price agreement with your customer, you are unable to pass that cost along and it will end up eroding your profit margin. This is an example of fixed price agreements working against you.

To minimize this risk, make sure that all agreements signed with customers have a clause allowing for increases in pricing due to factors beyond your control.

Interest Rate Risk

You are exposed to interest rate risk when you have financing with an interest rate that changes with changing market conditions, also called floating rate interest. For example, if you have a $100,000 operating loan with the bank at a floating interest rate currently at 7.5 percent, you will be paying $7,500 in interest a year (assuming no principal repayment). If interest rates go up by three quarters of a percent, you will now be paying 8.25 percent and your annual cost of borrowing will be $8,250. You are worse off when interest rates rise and better off when they fall.

It is difficult to predict interest rates and market conditions and this can make it difficult to predict cash flows. You may end up with a much higher interest expense than planned.

Businesses that are exposed to significant interest rate risk use a variety of means to hedge that risk, including interest rate swaps,

options, and forward contracts, all of which are beyond the scope of this book. Speak to your accountant for more information.

If you are exposed to only moderate interest rate risk, make sure that it is survivable. When projecting cash flows, look at "what if" scenarios. What would happen if interest rates went up by 1 percent? 5 percent? If your cash flows are tight in the start-up period and you cannot survive interest rate risk, make sure that all your debt financing is fixed rate.

Foreign Exchange Risk

This type of risk happens when the money coming into your business is denominated in a different currency than the money going out. For example, if you sell most of your product in yen and you pay most of your expenses in US dollars, you are better off when the US dollar falls against the yen and worse off when it rises. If both your revenues and your expenses are in the same currency, there is no risk because, if your revenues go up, your expenses go up and vice versa. This type of risk can squeeze your profit margins in much the same way a fixed price agreement or interest rate risk can.

It is impractical and unwise to simply avoid foreign sales because of the potential risk. There are many sophisticated hedging strategies that you can employ to minimize or get rid of the risk completely. To see an example of a currency option contract, please refer to the second book in the *Numbers 101 for Small Business* series, *Financial Management 101*.

Economic Dependence

If your business relies on one or only a few customers for all of its revenues, then your business is economically dependent. If losing one of your major customers would put your business in jeopardy, you are at risk of insolvency.

Economic dependence can be a difficult risk to eliminate, especially in the start-up years, when you may only start out with a few customers. Make sure that you continually seek new customers and new markets to make sure that you're not putting all your eggs in one basket.

Chapter Summary

➡ Along with the rewards in your business come many risks that you need to get a handle on and minimize.

➡ Securing loans with personal or business assets or with personal guarantees can get you a lower interest rate but expose you and your business to the risk of losing the assets.

➡ Fixed price agreements can lock you into an unfavorable arrangement unless properly structured.

➡ Interest rate and foreign exchange risk can squeeze profits and cause insolvency unless hedged.

Chapter

10

Home Sweet Home

Should you operate your business out of your home or should you rent or buy space? We look at the variables to consider.

Introduction

It's 8:30 in the morning. You're still in your pajamas, having just ushered your kids and spouse out the door to school and work, respectively. You take a moment to stack the breakfast dishes neatly in the dishwasher, then pour yourself another cup of coffee. Fifteen minutes later, you're showered and dressed in comfortable clothes and are checking your emails on your computer in the office set up in your spare bedroom. At 10:30 a.m., you stretch and grab another coffee, taking enough time to throw a load of laundry in the washer. Your 3:00 p.m. break allows you to put dinner in the oven and spend a little time with your children as they arrive home from school. It is the idyllic home office situation. Unfortunately, the reality is frequently very different than the dream.

Many entrepreneurs choose to start their small businesses out of their homes to begin with. This definitely saves money and can reduce the risk that would exist if they lock into a lease agreement on office space.

There are many considerations to keep in mind when you are deciding whether it makes sense to operate your business from your home or to lease office space. Some of these considerations are financial, while others relate to the effect of working from home on your personal life.

Does It Really Save Me Money?

When deciding whether or not to work from a home office, financial considerations come to the forefront, especially when you are first starting out. You are already paying all the expenses on your home whether or not you have your business there: the mortgage or rent, utilities, property taxes, maintenance, and a host of other costs. It may at first seem like it would be "free" to have your business operate out of your house. There are a few issues with that supposition, however:

- **Your house insurance may not cover a business.** You may have to get a separate insurance policy to cover the loss of business assets in your home or to cover the interruption in your business if something catastrophic happens, like a burst water pipe. This is an added expense that you will have to factor into your decision.

- **The zoning of your neighborhood may be residential only and may not allow a business to operate.** Check with your local zoning office to find out whether it's even possible for you to operate out of your home. Zoning officials will most likely ask you things like how many customers do you expect to have in the house and what type and how much parking you have available. You may have to pay extra fees or property taxes to the municipality in order to be able to operate a business.

CASE STUDY

Although EarthPower would have sales offices in Brussels and Atlanta, the management end would be run out of Craig's basement office until the company was able to find a suitable office space. Marnie was excited that her husband would be so close to home but Craig wondered if the arrangement would be feasible.

He got his answer soon enough. Unlike the home-based businesses of several of his college friends, Craig's home office arrangement worked very well. His partner spent much of his time in Brussels setting up the new sales office so Craig was left to build up the operational side. It would be at least six months before their projected cash flows would allow them to hire a full-time administrative assistant, so Craig was trying to split his time between telephone calls, bookkeeping, marketing, and on-shore sales.

The Tuesday before Thanksgiving, Craig "hit the wall." He was on a conference call with Brussels on the telephone. He was also speaking intermittently on his cell phone with a potential supplier from Charleston. The desk in front of him was piled high with typical business paperwork: invoices, billings, bank statements, gas receipts, and other assorted detritus. Craig ended his telephone conversation with Brussels and focused on his cell phone. He paced the floor as he spoke with the supplier, intentionally turning his back on the mountain of paperwork.

Then it happened. The business phone rang again. Craig felt his blood pressure rise. He was completely overwhelmed. It was then that Marnie appeared at the bottom of the basement stairs, a baby monitor in her hand. Craig knew that he couldn't handle family issues at the moment on top of everything else. He motioned to the cell phone, indicating he was busy but Marnie simply sat at the desk and answered the telephone.

"EarthPower Systems. This is Marnie." As she spoke to the caller, she extricated a notepad from the pile, picked up a pen from the floor and took notes. Craig could only stare as she ended the call, handed him the message slip, and picked up the leaning pile of papers on the desk, along with a long-neglected and dusty box of file folders, and disappeared back upstairs.

Marnie helped EarthPower organize its books and records and also answered the telephones when Craig's life got hectic (and when the baby was asleep). She would not have been able to do that if the business did not operate from their basement. The flexibility of the location allowed EarthPower resources that they would otherwise not have had.

- **You will be subsidizing the operating costs of your business.** This will definitely help to save money in the start-up phase of your business, but it may allow you to operate a business that wouldn't survive without that subsidy. Previously in this book, we discussed the fact that all businesses that are built on successful and sustainable models can pay all of their expenses and provide a return to the owners. Your business, if it is to be successful and have value that can be transferred to a buyer, must eventually be able to operate from leased or purchased premises. Not paying any premises expenses may lull you into thinking that your business is successful when it is truly not. If you work from home in the start-up period but plan on moving to a separate location in the future, make sure that you have tracked that cost in your cash flow projections.

How Will It Affect My Personal Life?

Once you have examined the financial considerations of whether to operate from your home, there are some practical issues that should be looked at as well.

The neighbors

Your neighbors might not be as enthused as you are about your new enterprise, especially if it results in increased traffic volumes on what would otherwise be a quiet residential street. If you run a business where you work from home but see your customers at their homes or places of business, you will not run into this issue.

If, on the other hand, you plan on having your customers come to your home office (and assuming your neighborhood is suitably zoned), it makes sense to discuss it with your neighbors first. You are not asking their permission; you are simply informing them as a courtesy and encouraging them to bring any concerns to your attention immediately instead of going to the municipality to complain. Who knows, your neighbors might end up being some of your best customers!

The on-call syndrome

When I first started my accounting and consulting practice from an office in my home, I thought I had set it up perfectly. All client meetings were by appointment only, so that I would always know when a client was coming. This gave me time to make sure my home office was tidy and that I was professionally dressed. My office hours were from 9:00 a.m. to 5:00 p.m. so that clients could call and reach me during those times.

That setup worked well for about the first week. But thereafter, clients started dropping in: "Well, I was just in the neighborhood and I knew you'd be here." Not only did this happen during the day, but also in the evenings and on weekends. I began to feel trapped in my own home, never being able to spend a lazy Saturday morning in my pajamas reading the newspaper or in my "grubby clothes" gardening in the yard for fear that there would be a knock at the door. Clients also called at all times of the day and night. I began to turn the ringer on the business telephone off at 5:00 p.m. so that I didn't have to ignore it.

Even if you set parameters on your availability, there is a probability that your customers will not always honor those limits. If you are the type of person who wants to create a distinct separation between your home life and your working life, you may not want to have a home office. If you do choose to have customers come to your home, here are some tips to make it easier on you and your family:

- Have a separate entrance for your home office. That way, if you do have unexpected customers, you do not have to traipse them through the kids' playroom and the kitchen stacked high with dirty dishes.

- Communicate your meeting and telephone policies with all of your customers. Make sure they understand what is acceptable and not acceptable. Put a sign on the office entrance door with your hours of operation and information on making appointments.

- Be firm but professional with customers who show up unexpectedly. Explain to them (once again) that they will need to make an appointment so that you can be more prepared for them.

- Have a separate telephone and fax line for the business from your home line. Turn off the ringer on the office telephone when outside of office hours. Record a telephone message reiterating your office hours and that you will be pleased to return the call during those hours.

The convenience

So far, we've looked mainly at the down side of working from home. For many entrepreneurs, however, this arrangement works well and allows them the flexibility to balance work and family responsibilities.

Having a home office will definitely save you commuting time, time that can be spent more effectively on managing and growing your business. It also can allow you to be home when your children get home from school, thereby saving on child care fees, or when service people have to come to your home to make repairs. If you can discipline yourself well enough, having a home office will let you structure your day more efficiently around family needs.

Willpower

When you work at an office outside the home, you have a clear divide between work time and home time. You know that when you are in the office, you are there for one reason: to work. This is not so clear when you have a home office, and if your willpower and ability to monitor yourself is weak, you may find yourself doing more lounging than working. Taking "just fifteen minutes" to catch "The Price Is Right" or to take a quick swim in the pool can often turn into the majority of the day.

To corral this problem, take some time first thing every morning to plan your day. Make a list of everything that you need and want to accomplish that day and prioritize them. Block time off in your calendar not only for your scheduled appointments but also to work on your tasks. For example, if you want to get a quote out to a customer by 5:00 p.m., block off an hour (if that's how long you think it will take) to work on the quote. This will help you make sure that you are not over-committing yourself and setting yourself up for failure. It also helps you to structure your day so that you are being as productive as you are able.

Chapter Summary

➡ There are many financial considerations involved in deciding whether working from a home office makes sense, including zoning, parking, and insurance.

➡ A home office can afford you more flexibility in balancing your home and work lives.

➡ It is important to be clear with your customers as to your available hours for telephone or face-to-face meetings.

➡ Working from home will require you to structure your time to ensure that you are being as productive as possible.

Chapter 11

Choosing Your External Team

No business survives for the long term without a great team of advisers; lawyers, accountants, financial planners, and a board of directors. We look at how to choose your advisory team and what questions you should be asking them.

Introduction

As you begin your new business, there will be no bigger factor in your success or failure than your choice of your business's advisers. Your lawyer, accountant, financial adviser, and board of directors will fill in the gaps in your own skills and will be valuable sources of information as you grow.

As a new entrepreneur, you may decide that this is an area in which you want to save money, it being the scarce resource that it is. I highly recommend, however, that you invest in good external advisers. A few hundred dollars now can save you a few thousand (or more!) later.

Chosen well, your external advisers can help you with the following:

- Provide guidance on your business's direction and growth strategy

- Connect you with lenders and investors to which you would otherwise have no knowledge of or way of approaching

- Find potential acquisition targets to fuel your business growth

- Troubleshoot roadblocks and other obstacles in which you lack experience

Finding the perfect fit in an adviser can seem like a daunting task when you're first starting out. You may find it difficult to know how to assess qualifications and experience. Let's have a look at your main group of advisers and what you will need to take into consideration when searching for the right ones.

Your Lawyer

You will need a lawyer to advise your small business on many issues, including the following:

- Incorporation
- Labor laws
- Contracts (with customers, suppliers, and employees)
- Mergers and acquisitions
- Estate planning matters
- Exit strategies
- Personal wills and powers of attorney

You will most likely start with a general practitioner who can handle most of the day-to-day legal work your business needs, and then hire specialists for everything else. A good general practitioner will have experience in many different areas and will know when to bring in a specialist. He or she will also be able to recommend one to you. Make sure that your prospective lawyer has experience with small businesses and doesn't mostly deal only with personal or family legal matters.

In the United States, each state has its own bar association that regulates the lawyers of that state. In Canada, the Canadian Bar Association regulates lawyers. These associations can help you find a lawyer in your community that specializes in small businesses.

Meet with him or her and assess how well the two of you communicate. Find out about his or her billing practices and whether a retainer (an amount of money paid in advance of work being undertaken) is required. Make sure to tell the lawyer about your personal situation as well so that he or she can see the whole picture and can make recommendations on wills, estates, and exit strategy planning.

Your Accountant

One of the areas that many entrepreneurs are weak in is finance and accounting. Their

---

CASE STUDY

"A board of directors? Are you serious?" Craig's partner, Gordon, looked at Vivian skeptically. "We're not Microsoft, you know."

Vivian said, "An independent board of directors is important for even the smallest of companies. A board can review your operations with a fresh set of eyes and perhaps find looming roadblocks or lucrative opportunities that you and Craig have missed because you both are so involved in the day-to-day operations of the company."

"Well," Craig said, "I guess it doesn't hurt to have a second opinion sometimes. I know we both feel like we're in over our heads at times."

"That's the purpose of a board of directors," said Vivian. "To help guide the company."

Craig turned to his partner. "What about John Wendsley?"

"The founder of Wendsley Motors?" Gordon asked. "He's retired now."

"I know. That's why he'd be perfect. He spent his lifetime building his business. Now he's retired and working on some volunteer projects. I think he might like to help out a new company," Craig said. "And he has an incredible amount of experience in building a business."

Vivian said, "That's a good start. Now let's make up a list of your potential board members and plan how we're going to present the opportunity to them."

backgrounds have generally not allowed them sufficient exposure to this critical foundation wall of any business.

The right accountant can help you in several areas:

- Selecting and setting up your record keeping system
- Developing your monthly management operating plan
- Defining your key success factors
- Preparing cash flow projections
- Tax planning
- Exit strategy planning
- Mergers and acquisitions
- Human resource interviewing and screening
- Growth strategies
- Estate planning

As you can see, accountants are far more than "bean counters." But how do you know when you have found the right one? Here are some strategies to help you select an accountant:

1. **Talk to your business associates.** They can be a great source of referral for an accountant. Ask your associates not only questions about the competency of the accountant but also about their relationship. Ultimately, you will need an accountant that speaks the language of the small-business owner, not "accountant talk."

2. **Review the websites of the professional accounting bodies in your jurisdiction.** Each professional organization will have regulated training and experience requirements that individuals will have to perform before receiving their professional designation. Remember, too, that the word "accountant" is not regulated the way the word

"lawyer" is. Anyone can call himself or herself an accountant and prepare financial statements and tax returns. It's important to delve into the qualifications of the person you're about to hire.

In the United States, professional accountants are called Certified Public Accountants (CPAs) and are regulated by the American Institute of Certified Public Accountants (www.aicpa.org). In Canada, chartered accountants are regulated by the Canadian Institute of Chartered Accountants (www.cica.ca), certified management accountants are regulated by the Society of Management Accountants of Canada (www.cma-canada.org), and certified general accountants are regulated by the Certified General Accountants Association of Canada (www.cga-canada.org).

Each of these designations carries with them differing levels of training and experience requirements. The websites can also direct you to local members.

3. **Meet with the prospective accountant.** This initial "get to know you" meeting should come at no charge to you, but ask if that's the case ahead of time. In the years to come, you will have to be able to communicate well with the accountant, understand what he or she is telling you, and trust the information being imparted to you. Never underestimate your feelings about the accountant at this first meeting. You should feel that the two of you "click." At this meeting you should also discuss the accountant's areas of expertise, number of clients (you don't want to be the first client

but you also don't want to be a tiny fish in an ocean), and billing policies and rates.

4. **Ask for references.** The accountant should be able to give you the names of several small-business clients similar to yourself that you can call and ask questions about their relationship with the accountant. Note that because of confidentiality issues, the accountant will first have to get permission from the clients to use them as references.

As with all of your advisers, don't rush into hiring an accountant. Take your time and it will certainly pay off in the long run.

Your Financial Adviser

In most jurisdictions, the term "financial planner" is as unregulated as "accountant." Anyone can call himself or herself a financial planner. Of all your advisers, your choice of financial planner can have the greatest impact on your personal and business wealth.

What do financial planners actually do for you? It depends on whom you choose, but most financial planners can do the following:

- Draw up an investment plan for your retirement

- Recommend the mix of investments that your portfolio should have

- Recommend specific investments and even be able to purchase them on your behalf

- Help you determine your insurance needs

- Recommend other financial products, such as mortgages and tax-deferred shelters

- Help you invest excess profits from your business

It is critical to find an accountant and financial planner who work well together. Their areas of expertise will overlap and it's important that they're on the same page. All tax strategies recommended by your financial planner should be agreed to by your accountant and any investment strategy organized by your accountant should be vetted by your financial planner. Once you find an accountant that you trust, he or she is likely a good source of recommendation for a financial planner.

It's also important to find an independent planner. This means that the planner is not connected to nor gets paid by investment companies. You want to make sure that the planner is working in your best interest, not the best interest of lining his or her pocket. Financial planners get paid in different ways depending upon how they operate and the size and type of portfolio you have:

- **Commissions.** Some planners receive commissions from the mutual fund and insurance companies whose products are sold through them. For example, with this type of arrangement, if you were to purchase $10,000 worth of mutual fund units through your planner, the fund company would pay the planner a commission. You would not have to pay anything. Although this seems like a good idea for you, it may not be in the long run if the planner is simply recommending the product on which he or she receives the most commission. In this type of fee arrangement, it's important to find a planner who deals with multiple companies and can "shop your business around" for you, much like an insurance broker.

- **Hourly fee.** Some planners work much like accountants and lawyers and will charge you by the hour to work on your financial plan.

- **Asset-based fees.** Some planners will charge a fee based on a percentage (usually half to 1 percent) of the assets in your portfolio to manage that portfolio. This generally only happens if you have a large portfolio.

Once you have decided upon your financial planner, make sure you meet with him or her at least annually to review the financial plan. Your planner can explain the growth in your assets in the previous year based on what has happened in world markets, and can review the plan to make sure that you are still on track for the upcoming year.

Your Board of Directors

When you think of the phrase "board of directors," mammoth companies like Microsoft and General Motors probably spring immediately to mind. Every corporation, however, regardless of size, is required to maintain a board of directors. Even if your business is not incorporated, it is advisable to have at least an informal board.

The board of directors is a slate of advisers chosen by the shareholders of the company to advise and guide management. Especially in larger companies, the board is mostly made up of external members, that is to say those that do not also work in the company. They may be business owners or managers themselves. The incorporation documents of the company outline the board's duties and responsibilities, including which issues must be voted on by the board.

In a small company, getting external board members may be difficult, but it is even more critical than for a larger organization. Experienced board members bring knowledge and advisory skills to the table that you may lack. If nothing else, they bring new ideas and opinions.

So why would someone want to sit on your board of directors? Certainly not for the cold hard cash. Fewer than 50 percent of companies pay their boards, and those that do, pay a pittance. Most directors sit on boards for the pleasure of helping guide a fledgling company, the same reason that you're an entrepreneur.

To find your directors, start by making a list of those business owners and managers in your community whom you trust and respect and who are not afraid of voicing their opinions. For this reason, you will not want to include friends and family as they may be too concerned with hurting your feelings to tell you that you are driving the company into the ground. Speak with those on your list about your need for guidance in your new venture. Even those who choose to decline the offer of being on the board may extend other offers, such as being available to offer advice or hooking you up with investors and lenders.

One last word about directors. The directors of a corporation are legally liable for everything the company does, which may be one reason that those on your list shy away from the responsibility. There is a type of insurance product that provides some protection to the directors and your directors may insist that you take out such a policy, so make sure that you calculate the premiums into your cash flows.

Chapter Summary

➡ Your team of external advisers is made up of your lawyer, accountant, financial planner, and board of directors.

➡ The main role of your external advisers is to fill in the gaps in your knowledge and experience so that your business can avoid pitfalls and flourish.

➡ One of the best ways to find your accountant and lawyer is through speaking with other small-business owners in your community.

➡ Your board of directors will be charged with the task of guiding the company in all major decisions and should be chosen carefully.

Chapter

12

Assessing the Competition

In this chapter, we turn to competitive analysis. What are the other companies in your industry doing well? Doing badly?

Introduction

What first comes to mind when you hear the phrase "competitive intelligence"? Slinking around in the bushes with a pair of binoculars and a notepad, eating stale donuts and drinking cold coffee, hoping for a single glimpse of something illusive and perhaps illicit? Or a James Bond-type character dressed to kill and sipping a martini (shaken not stirred), snapping pictures of forbidden foreign documents with a cufflink camera? Well, unfortunately, the real world of competitive intelligence isn't nearly as glamorous as all that.

Competitive intelligence is something that every smart entrepreneur does on a continual basis. It is simply the process of uncovering, analyzing, and presenting publicly available information on your business's competitors in order to maintain a competitive advantage in the marketplace.

In Chapter 5, we looked at preparing the business plan, in which you outline your business's niche and position in the industry. Competitive intelligence is the tool to research the background information. As the owner and manager (and chief bottle washer) of your business, the competitive intelligence job will most likely fall to you. It becomes an integral part of your ongoing analysis of your own operations as well as the entire operating environment. Competitive intelligence will tell you what products or services you should be offering, how you can present them to existing and potential customers, and how to improve your position in your industry relative to your competitors.

Let's have a look at the steps to take in order to analyze your competition.

Identify the Competition

Do you know who your competitors are? Start by opening the telephone book and scanning the Yellow Pages or the business directory. If you are a bookstore, your most direct competitors are the other bookstores in your local area. They will all be listed alongside your business in the telephone book.

Your list of competitors stretches beyond the list of direct competitors, however. It includes those providers who can deliver the same product or service as you do through another distribution channel, such as over the internet or through trade shows. Staying with the bookstore example, it would mean that you are also in competition with amazon.com, for example.

Your competitors also include businesses that can deliver a different product or service that accomplishes the same goal. This means that your bookstore must not only compete for book business but for entertainment business.

You are competing with movie theaters, dance clubs, and cable networks.

Having a solid understanding of the competitors in your market will help you to better understand your own business and its place in the competitive environment.

What Do They Do Right and Wrong?

Once you have determined who the competition is, it's time to evaluate what is working for them and against them.

Start a file on each of your major competitors. Gather as much of their marketing, promotional, and sales material as possible. Print off pages from their website. Cut out display ads from the newspaper and magazines. Listen to their speeches and presentations.

Review all of the printed material. What kind of image is this competitor portraying? If you were a potential customer, what would

---

CASE STUDY

"Tell me about Green Source Inc.," Vivian said the next day when she and the two partners met again.

Craig shrugged his shoulders. "I don't know. They're a new company based out of Atlanta. They seem to be selling the same types of products we are, but I haven't been paying much attention to them."

Gordon chimed in. "If we pay too much attention to them, it'll look like we're scared."

Vivian said, "On the contrary. Paying close attention to your competition is what smart companies do. You can learn lots from finding out how they're approaching potential customers, what their marketing message is, and what their pricing looks like."

"But we don't want to copy them," Craig protested. "We want to be the market leader."

"How will you know if you're leading if you don't know who's following you and where they are in the race?" asked Vivian. "You have to understand your competition inside and out and be able to articulate what your market niche is compared to theirs and how your products and services are superior."

"They're running a seminar on wind power over at the Arena next Wednesday. Do you think we should go?" asked Craig.

Vivian said, "I think that's a good start. Then, let's make a list of all the things we want to know about the competition and we'll list ideas about how to obtain that information."

attract you to this business? What type of customer are they trying to appeal to? Is it exactly the same market as you are targeting or are they appealing to a customer base you haven't before contemplated? Do they have products or services that you don't offer your customers? Do they use better technology and equipment than you do?

Where is this business weak? Is their location difficult to find? Are they understaffed? Overpriced?

Call the business as if you were a potential customer. How are you greeted when you call? Are they helpful and friendly or indifferent?

As you go through this process with each of your major competitors, do not discount your feelings about the business. Customers will make their buy/don't buy decision based on their immediate perceptions of a business, so keep in mind what perceptions you are forming from your analysis.

How Are They Positioned to Take Advantage of Opportunities?

Opportunities occur outside the control of a business. Each business will be differently positioned to be able to take advantage of these opportunities. For example, if one of your new competitors is highly leveraged (that is to say, has bought a lot of equipment and tools on credit), they may not be able to buy an existing business if one suddenly comes up for sale. How are your competitors positioned to be able to take advantage of new technology in your industry? Will they be able to retool in time to capture new customer bases or are they already sinking under their management structure?

How Vulnerable Are They to Changing Market Conditions?

The other side of being able to take advantage of opportunities is being able to react to external threats. Threats can include things like changing tax laws, legal action, new competitors, and theft — all things that are potential land mines for businesses that are not prepared.

Does the structure of your competitors hinder their ability to respond to threats? For example, if you are in the tire recycling business, how would each of your competitors be able to deal with new regulations restricting the storage of used tires? Would some be out of business?

How Do You Stack Up?

The ultimate goal of collecting all of this competitive information is to be able to use it to your advantage. Compare yourself to your competitors based on your research, and answer these questions:

1. Are there other products or services I should be offering my customers?

2. Should I offer higher quality products or services?

3. Are there other customer groups I should be targeting?

4. How can we improve our customer service to make our customers more loyal?

5. What can we improve in our marketing, promotional, and sales materials to better communicate who we are to our customers?

6. Should we be upgrading our equipment to be able to save us money or produce more efficiently?

7. Should we be accepting more forms of payment to make it easier for our customers to pay us?

8. Can we pursue more free media attention?

9. Are there networking opportunities that we should be pursuing?

10. How can we position ourselves to be better able to capitalize on opportunities and weather threats?

Competitive analysis is an ongoing process of keeping apprised of the ever-changing nature of the market in which you operate. You need to regularly monitor your competitors to see how they evolve and grow. If they're smart, they'll be monitoring you too!

SWOT ANALYSIS

In MBA-speak, the analysis we discussed above is called a SWOT analysis:

Strengths

Weaknesses

Opportunities

Threats

A business's strengths and weaknesses are those qualities internal to the business, those things that are under the business's control. Opportunities and threats come from the external operating environment and are events to which the business must react.

A SWOT analysis helps a business to identify its best and worst qualities and allows the business to have a deeper understanding of how to find opportunities and weather threats.

Competitive Analysis

One way to keep all of your competitive analysis organized is to set up a binder with a section for each of your major competitors. Keep the summary research all on one page for each competitor and file their marketing, promotional, and sales material in behind. You may wish to use or modify Worksheet 2 to do a competitive analysis for your business.

Intelligence Resources

With the advent of the web, it is easier than ever to research your competitors. Here are some resources that you can use to assist your research:

- **Web search engines,** such as Google (www.google.com). In a search engine, you simply type in the words that you are looking for and the engine lists all of the web pages that contain those words. You will frequently have to narrow down your search to make sure that you are getting the most relevant results. You may find links to your competitor's website, advertising, and upcoming event listings, and chat rooms where customers are discussing the product or service.

- **News monitoring or Web clipping services.** Some of these services are free and some are subscription based. News monitoring services scour the Web for news articles containing words that you specify. You can request, for example, that you be notified when there are articles or news stories generated that contain the words "Microsoft Corp."

- **Corporate website.** Many businesses maintain their own websites. Some of these sites are simply an online representation of the business brochure. On

WORKSHEET 2
COMPETITIVE ANALYSIS

Business name:

Address:

Contacts:

Years in business:

Products or services:

Pricing structure

Strengths	Weaknesses

Opportunities	Threats

Other notes:

some, you can order products or services, ask questions, and drill down into the details of products or services being offered. Your competitors' websites will give you a good idea of how the businesses present themselves and what they perceive to be their strengths. If your competitors don't have websites, you may wish to consider developing one for your business to give you a competitive advantage.

Chapter Summary

➡ Competitive intelligence is the gathering, analyzing, and using of publicly available information about the competitors in your industry.

➡ Research and analysis of your competitors includes gathering all marketing, promotional, and sales material as well as visiting the business and attending speeches and events hosted by the business.

➡ Competitive intelligence is an ongoing process to continually monitor the ever-changing nature of the environment in which you operate.

➡ There are many Internet-based tools that you can incorporate into your competitive analysis process.

Chapter 13

Forecasting Profit

A re you going to be able to meet payroll next week? Make the interest and principal payments on your business loans next month? We look at how to forecast and plan cash flows for smooth sailing.

Introduction

In earlier chapters, we discussed how you will forecast your cash flow to ascertain whether your business idea is a good one and also to be able to present information to lenders and investors.

In this chapter, we will talk about continual forecasting, that is, how to make sure that your business is both making a profit and providing positive cash flow to finance growth and expansion. You will need this information to know if you're on track with your plan and also to be able to attract new sources of financing. There are a number of areas to focus on to ensure that your cash management stays an important part of your business.

Keep Your Bookkeeping Up-to-Date

If you're like most small-business owners, this probably isn't the most fun or fulfilling part of your job, but it is definitely the most critical. The only way that you will be able to accurately predict your financing needs is by tracking your business's current performance. Keeping accurate records will also tell you which suppliers need to be paid to avoid penalties and interest, and which customers are overdue in their payments. Make sure you set aside some time every day to record the bookkeeping for the prior day.

Always Forecast a Rolling 12 Months

When you first started your business, you prepared a 12-month and 5-year cash flow projection. The 12-month projection should be a living, breathing entity, which you will update on a monthly basis. The term "rolling" 12 months simply means that as one month drops into history, you will project out another one. For example, if it's now February 2008, your 12-month projection will encompass March 2008 to February 2009. In March 2008, the projection will drop March 2008 (as it has already happened) and add in March 2009. With this method, you will always know what lies ahead for the next 12 months. The projection will warn you if you are going to run out of cash at any point in the next year. Then you can prepare by sourcing financing to cover the shortfall rather than be startled by it when your bank balance is zero.

Tighten Up Billing and Collection Policies

Managing your operating funds is critical to every small business and lack of control over these issues sinks a good number of businesses. Take some time to review your billing and credit policies. Are they in line with your competitors? Do you extend credit too freely? Too stingily? How are the receivables being followed up? Is it being done consistently?

If you find that receivables management tends to be one of the last things you hastily do, you may want to consider hiring an accounts receivable clerk to manage the funds coming in. It's critical to make sure that the money comes in as regularly as you have predicted in your cash flow statement. You can have a highly profitable business and still go bankrupt because customers aren't paying you on time. For a more in-depth discussion of accounts receivable policies, please refer to the second book in the *Numbers 101 for Small Business* series, *Financial Management 101*.

Hire Someone to Do It If You Can't

As you will quickly learn in operating your business, you can't do everything, although small-business owners give it their best shot. You will have to continually analyze the consequences of things falling through the cracks. For example, if accounts payable isn't done regularly, you may be incurring significant penalties and interest on late payments or NSF checks. If you have too much work for one person to do, you could be losing customers. If you don't keep up with your forecasting, you may suddenly run out of cash. Know when to hire someone and what you most need done. For a more in-depth discussion of hiring, please refer to Chapter 14.

Keep on Top of Changes in the Operating Environment

In Chapter 12, we discussed assessing your competition, their internal strengths and weaknesses, and how they will be able to react to external opportunities and threats. It's every bit as important for you to continually analyze the environment in which your business operates and assess how you are positioned to take advantage of opportunities and deal with roadblocks.

Formalize this analysis as part of your day. Stay on top of changes in the industry by reading industry publications and networking with other small-business owners, both those in your particular industry and those who operate businesses in the same community as you. Join your local Chamber of Commerce to find out what's happening in the world of small business. Talk to your accountant about pending changes in tax and audit laws.

The more informed you are, the better you will be able to finance the future.

Keep the Work Coming In

You may sometimes feel that you will be fine once you finish the mound of work you have on your plate right now and can rest for a few minutes. One very serious mistake made frequently by small-business owners is to concentrate only on today's work without considering where the work will come from tomorrow. As a small-business owner, you have three heads: one that looks back to the past to learn from history, one that's focused on the here and now and the things that need to be accomplished today, and one that looks to the future, to figure out what work needs to be generated in order to meet your revenue targets.

Always keep an eye on future work. It's only work that gets brought in, done, billed, and collected that will result in cash in your bank account. Make sure that there are no gaps in that stream of cash.

Continually Assess New Sources of Financing

Once you have your initial source of financing in place, you may think that your need for cash has ended, but a wise entrepreneur always has his or her eye on the financial markets. You may need to replace your initial source of financing some day and you will need to know what the new cost of capital will be because it will affect your cash flow projections. You may have a sudden opportunity to purchase another business in your industry and will want to have already done your homework with respect to sources and cost of capital.

Make sure you spend time talking with your accountant and your financial planner about your existing and projected cash needs. They may be able to help you with your future needs.

Chapter Summary

➡ Cash flow projections should be an ongoing and integral part of your management operating plan.

➡ Keeping your historical financial bookkeeping up to date is critical to being able to predict future problems.

➡ Assess the need to hire an employee to help keep you on top of financial recording and planning if you are unable to do it by yourself.

➡ Continually assess new sources of financing in case you need to replace your existing funding or need money for expansion.

Chapter
14

Investing in Labor

Without your staff, your business wouldn't exist. But when is it time to hire? Will another employee pay for himself or herself? We look at the issues surrounding getting the most out of your investment in your employees.

Introduction

If you start out like most small businesses, there will be only you in the beginning. You will be the manager, sales director, administration assistant, and office cleaner. As your business grows, you will be constantly assessing whether you will be better off to hire an employee or to simply work harder and reap more of the profits for yourself.

The decision process for hiring labor is much like the process for any other type of capital investment. I use the term "capital investment" because the cost of an employee is not like most other operating expenses you will incur, but is more like an investment. You will spend money to "purchase" the labor, but will receive a greater return on investment over time than the amount originally invested. For example, if it costs you $30,000 a year to hire an employee, and he or she is able to bill out $47,000 of his or her time to your customers, you are receiving a 57 percent return on your investment.

The decision is rarely as cut and dried as this, however. Frequently, employees need to be hired in advance of the expected increase in revenues and the question then becomes, when is the right time? You don't want to incur unnecessary expenses on the one hand, but you also don't want to work yourself into an early grave on the other. This chapter looks at some of the considerations to ponder when deciding whether or not and when to hire.

The Cost of an Employee

When assessing how much it will cost you to hire an employee, it's important to take into consideration all of the costs involved, including some of the following.

Salary

This is the most obvious one. It is the amount that you quote to the employee when hiring. Wages can be either in the form of a fixed annual salary (e.g., $25,000 per year), or an hourly rate (e.g., $7.50 per hour). If you plan on paying hourly, you will need to estimate how many hours the employee will work in a standard year. A typical work year is around 1,950 hours, taking into account holidays and vacation time.

The quoted salary or hourly rate will not end up being the amount the employee pockets however. Depending upon the jurisdiction in which you operate, you may be required to deduct income taxes, pension contributions, unemployment premiums, or health care premiums. This does not matter to your calculations, however, as you will be spending the entire amount, even though you will be giving some to the government.

Employer taxes

In some jurisdictions, you will be required to pay additional amounts to the government for pension, unemployment, and health care premiums on top of what you have withheld from your employee. These amounts are usually based on the dollar amount of your total payroll. Ask your accountant for the amounts and rates and be sure to take these additional costs into account.

Office space

When you hire an employee, you will need to have a space for him or her to work in as well as additional office supplies and equipment, like a desk, workbench, telephone, and computer. List out all of these additional items that you will need for a new employee and estimate the cost.

You may instead decide to have your employee work from his or her own home. This is called telecommuting. This is one way that you can lower your labor costs and still get the help you need.

Fringe benefits

In order to attract quality employees, small-business owners make their businesses more attractive to potential employees by offering benefits other than salary. These benefits might

---

CASE STUDY

"We've got to spend more time developing the US market," Craig's partner, Gordon, said.

"I know we do but I'm just snowed under with all of the administrative details. And you're always in Europe." Craig poured a cup of coffee. "Even with Marnie helping out, we're still way too busy."

"I think it's time we hire a full-time office manager," Gordon said.

"But it's too early; we didn't plan to do that until month six," Craig said.

"Just think about the potential sales we're losing because you're stuck doing all the paperwork. Let's rework the cash flows assuming that you'll be able to spend 80 percent of your time talking with potential customers."

Later that afternoon, Craig reviewed the projections. "We could have doubled our sales if I had been able to spend more time with potential customers. Trying to save money really got us behind."

Gordon said, "Well, let's start the process of hiring an office manager now. Then we can get back on track."

include health care, life insurance, gym memberships, baseball or hockey tickets, and a host of other incentives. If you will be offering any of these to your employees, calculate and factor in the cost of these additional benefits.

Calculating the Benefit

Now that you know how much it will cost to hire an employee, what will be the benefit to your business? This will partly be determined by what role the employee will play in the business. It is easier to calculate the benefit if the employee will be directly connected to the production of the product or service. For example, if you are hiring another hairstylist, you can compare the cost of the new stylist to the projected revenues that he or she will bring in. It's a much more difficult task to calculate the benefit of hiring a receptionist, who is critical to the successful operation of your business but doesn't directly bring revenues in the door.

Let's have a look at each of these types of employees.

Direct labor

This type of employee will actually do some of the work that the business does. He or she will be building widgets or providing services to your customers. To calculate the benefit of hiring direct labor, estimate how many units the employee can make of the product or how many hours he or she can bill out.

Here's an example.

Roland runs a computer consulting business. He is frequently out on service calls to residential customers who need repairs to their computers or training on new software. Roland is working 60 hours a week and his booking lag is growing. He frequently can't get out to a customer's home within a week of the call and he is losing business because of it.

He has decided to look into hiring another technician in order to be able to handle more service calls. The going rate is $39,450 for a technician, which includes all peripheral expenses. Roland is certain that he can keep the new technician busy full time, both from the current customer base and the new customers that will be pursued when Roland once again has time for marketing. Roland will charge the new tech out at the same rate he charges himself out: $35 per hour. Roland estimates that of the 1,950 hours available in a year, he can bill the technician out for 90 percent of them, or 1,755 hours. The estimated revenue from hiring the new technician will therefore be:

1,755 hours X $35 per hour = $61,425

Roland would therefore make a 56 percent return on his investment in a new technician and he would be farther ahead to hire one than to keep going on as before. Roland can also calculate how many hours he will have to bill the technician out at to break even on his investment:

Break even = $39,450 ÷ $35 per hour = 1,127 hours

Therefore, Roland would only have to bill the new technician out for 58 percent of the available hours before he would be worse off.

Indirect labor

This type of employee isn't directly responsible for generating revenues in the business, but is critical to its success. These types of positions might include receptionists, bookkeepers, marketing directors, or delivery people. It's more difficult to quantify the contribution of these employees. Let's look at an example to see how we might do it.

Zoe runs an editing service for small businesses. So far, she's been the sole employee and has performed all of the functions of the business by herself. She has started to notice that she can't keep up with the telephone calls from customers and potential customers and that she is losing business because of it. She estimates that she currently spends 50 percent of her time in actual billable work (at $55 per hour), 40 percent of her time on reception and administration duties, and the other 10 percent of her time on management. Zoe wants to look into the possibility of hiring an office manager to answer telephones and perform most of the administrative duties that Zoe is currently doing. How can we estimate the value of a new employee?

We can look at it from the perspective of what Zoe will gain in productivity. She will be gaining back 40 percent of her time, which she can theoretically bill out to customers. So:

(1,950 hours per year X 40%) X $55 billing rate = $42,900

Therefore, if the cost of an administrative assistant is less than $42,900, Zoe is better off by hiring one than to keep going alone. Zoe will also benefit by retaining more customers and building her customer base, so that, in time, she will be positioned to hire another editor (direct labor).

Your Billing Multiplier

Your billing multiplier is another method of determining when the time is right to hire direct labor. It is calculated by dividing your business's revenues by your direct labor cost. For example, if your revenues are $150,000 and your direct labor cost is $51,250, the billing multiplier is 2.93. The higher the multiple, the more revenues you are earning per unit of labor.

You can compare your multiple to the industry average or to your own multiple over time. To find out what the average is for your industry, start by speaking with your industry association to see if they maintain such statistics. Your accountant may also be able to tell you what's usual. You can track your own multiple over time and, once you have some financial history in your business, you'll be able to tell at what point the multiple tells you that it's time to hire again.

Five Signs It's Time to Hire

Here are five indicators that you may be in a good position to hire someone:

1. **The backlog of work is growing.** If you are noticing that customers must endure longer than average wait times, it may be time to bring someone new on board before customer service levels decline.

2. **Your billing multiplier is rising.** See the above detailed discussion of the billing multiplier.

3. **Your productivity level and that of your existing employees is dropping.** This may be due to "burnout" from trying to work too hard for too long a period of time.

4. **You are well capitalized for growth.** The worst thing that could happen is for you to attract new business with the added employee and not be able to fund the growth.

5. **The pay for overtime is increasing.** If you're finding that you are regularly paying existing staff for working overtime, it's an indication that you may need a new employee. Employees who work chronic overtime are less productive and more prone to burning out.

Chapter Summary

➡ Spending on labor is more like an investment in capital than an operating expense, as ou will expect to receive a return on that investment.

➡ When calculating the cost of an employee, make sure to take into consideration all of the peripheral expenses: payroll taxes, fringe benefits, and additional office space and supplies.

➡ Calculating the benefit of hiring a direct labor employee is easier than with an indirect labor employee, but both calculations are important.

➡ If your billing multiplier is high compared to your industry average or to your historical multiplier, it may indicate the need to hire an employee.

Chapter

15

Investing in Equipment

Most businesses require equipment to operate, be it computers or rototillers or printing presses. This chapter reviews the balancing of the costs versus the benefits of buying equipment.

Introduction

In most small businesses, the purchase or lease of equipment will be the largest expenditure in the cash flows. As a small-business owner, you will continually be assessing whether to repair or replace old equipment or invest in new equipment. You will be balancing your limited resources (your existing equipment) against your even more limited resource (cash). In the world of financial management, this is called capital budgeting. The term is not important but the concept is. Once you have decided what products and services your business will offer, your job is to ensure that the business does that in the most cost-effective manner, making the most efficient use of equipment.

Equipment encompasses many varied things in a small business. It includes the machinery that your business needs to produce its products, such as metal stamping equipment, injection molds, or table saws. It also includes peripheral equipment, that is, equipment not directly used in the production of goods but important none the less (e.g., computers, cellular telephones, vehicles, and software).

Let's have a look at how we might approach the decision-making process.

To Buy or Not to Buy

The main purpose of any investment is to create value for the investor. Why else would he or she spend the money in the first place?

Let's look at the example of a car. Suppose you're at an estate auction one day and you find a beat-up, paint-chipped 1970 Ford Mustang that, despite its less-than-ideal appearance, runs well. You buy it for $5,000. Your spouse, of course, thinks that you have absolutely lost your mind, but something tells you there is value in the car. You have a friend who does body work and you pay her $3,000 to work on the body and repaint the car. You spend another $200 vacuuming and shampooing the interior and having the car waxed. In total, you have spent $8,200 on the car. You place an ad in the local paper under "Collectible Cars" and you sell the car the next week for $11,000. You have basically been the manager or general contractor of this project and have brought together raw materials (the car) and labor and supplies to create an additional value of $2,800 ($11,000 − $8,200). You are able to pocket the $2,800 and you walk away happy.

The capital budgeting decision tries to identify *before* the investment is made whether there is positive value in a project. When we look at the decision whether or not to purchase equipment, we want to make sure that the purchase will add net value (and net positive cash flows) to the business. In our car example, if we had accurately projected the costs and the revenue from selling the car, we would have calculated the $2,800 in net value. It was easy in that situation as the expenses and revenue happened quite close together in time. With equipment budgeting decisions, the expenses and revenues happen over a longer period of time, so we are comparing today's dollars with future dollars. As we have seen in previous chapters, a dollar in the future is worth less than a dollar today, so we need to look at the discounted cash flows to be able to compare all of the inflows and outflows of cash in the same time frame.

The challenge that we face in capital budgeting is that we can only estimate the future revenue stream (cash inflows). If we estimate incorrectly, we may undertake to purchase equipment that ends up costing us more in the long run than the positive benefits it generates. On the other hand, the equipment that we purchase will most likely be financed, either through bank loans or leases. The expense side of the decision is fixed and, whether or not the new equipment generates the expected revenue levels, bank loans and the lease must be repaid. Therefore, adding leveraged fixed assets to your business involves risk. Careful and accurate estimating and decision analysis can help to soften that risk.

Let's have a look at some of the factors to consider when planning for your equipment purchase.

Erosion

In some business situations, purchasing new equipment allows you to offer new products and services to new groups of customers. This will have a direct positive effect on your revenue stream. On the other hand, where your existing customers will buy the new products and services instead of the old ones, your new equipment will eat into or erode your existing revenue streams. This erosion must be taken into account when estimating your new purchase.

Financing

Especially in the start-up phase of business, your equipment purchases will most likely be financed through a bank loan or through capital leases. Although undertaking these purchases will result in an increase in assets, it will also result in an increase in debt load. This will affect many of your financial statement ratios, including current ratio (current assets ÷ current liabilities) and debt to equity (debt ÷ equity). (For a more in-depth discussion of ratio analysis, please refer to the second book in the *Numbers 101 for Small Business* series, *Financial Management 101*.)

It's important to analyze the entire impact of the purchase. Will you be offside on your bank loan if you increase your debt load? How involved are the other investors in your business supposed to be in the decision? Do you need consensus? What kind of rate can you borrow at to buy this equipment? Frequently, lease rates are difficult to ascertain, so you may need to speak with your accountant about your pending asset purchase to ensure that you are getting the best possible lending rate.

Risk

When assessing the discounted cash flows, the theoretical rule is that you would proceed with any project that has positive discounted cash flows (that is to say, you'll be creating value with those projects). However, in real life, you only have so much cash so it would be impossible to invest in all of the equipment that would make you more money. You have to choose among various projects to find not only the greatest return, but also the least risk.

For example, let's say you own a small bookbinding company with three employees. You are looking to increase your revenues through the purchase of printing equipment. You have $10,000 in financing available. You have found two projects that you feel would help to grow your business, but they are mutually exclusive as each would require a $10,000 investment.

The first option is to purchase another press similar to the one you currently run except that it will be able to print 50 percent faster. This will allow you to run the same types of jobs as you have in the past but you will be able to take on larger orders and larger customers because of the increase in capacity.

The second option is to purchase an on-demand print machine that can produce single copies of books. This is an emerging technology and would allow customers to produce small runs of their self-published books and thereby make publishing a more affordable activity for these types of authors. There are only a few dozen of these "self-serve" type machines in the country and you would be on the leading edge of the technology.

If the expected revenue and cost profiles from both of these investments are exactly the same, you would most likely choose the first one if your main goal was risk reduction. You are comfortable with the technology you currently have and an increase to your capacity would almost certainly increase the bottom line. On the other hand, the new technology used in the second option is unproven and therefore your revenue increase estimates will be softer. The risk of loss from the new product is higher.

However, if your main goal is to be a market leader, you will most likely choose the second option: Higher risk but with a greater chance of capturing market share and becoming a leader in the new technology. Once the financial pros and cons have been weighed, the risk and other non-financial facets of the proposals (such as your goals as an entrepreneur) must be considered.

Chapter Summary

→ As a small-business owner, you will be continually deciding whether to repair existing equipment or buy new.

→ Discounted cash flows is the method used most frequently to assist with the decision about whether investing in new equipment will pay off.

→ A small business's cash resources are finite, so it is impossible to choose all equipment investments that produce positive discounted cash flow.

→ There are many peripheral considerations to take into account other than net cash flows, such as the erosion on the existing revenue stream, the impact on existing financing, and the risk involved in reaping the projected reward.

Chapter
16

Financing Expansion

W hen is it time to grow and where will the money come from to do that? We look at how to make a business case for growth.

Introduction

Every small-business owner contemplates expanding at one stage of operations or another. Once you have had proven success with your business model, it's natural to think about how much more profit you can make using your entrepreneurial skills. Expanding your business has the potential to provide you with some or all of the following:

- **Economies of scale.** You may be able to add customers and revenue without increasing or expanding your current resources.

- **Increased profile.** Becoming a larger business may give you more stature in

the community and may attract larger customers.

- **Increased sales.** These may potentially (but not always) lead to greater profits.

- **Decreased risk.** If you are concerned about being economically dependent on a few large customers, expansion can provide the diversity of clientele needed to mitigate that risk.

- **Greater personal fulfillment.** You know that your business model works and can not only support you, but can become even larger.

Some entrepreneurs dream of expanding their business. Others may be happy to grow their business to a certain size and then hold the fort, balancing work and other lifestyle issues. The decision to expand is based upon both financial and non-financial considerations.

Let's first have a look at the different types of expansion that you might contemplate.

Horizontal Expansion

Horizontal expansion means increasing your revenues from the same type of business as you are already in. There are five main ways to expand horizontally.

Increase your capacity

You can add new equipment, either more of the same type of equipment as you already have or new technology that will perform the same function less expensively and more efficiently. Increasing capacity would also include adding more staff to be able to handle higher sales volumes or renting or buying new office or warehouse space.

Expand your geographic area

You might choose to sell your products or services farther afield, either with a sales force, new bricks and mortar locations, or via the Internet. You may also consider translating your packaging and advertising to be able to service foreign markets.

Develop new products or services

You may choose to increase your revenues by adding new products or services to your offerings. These products and services can be marketed to your existing customer base or to new markets. This is usually referred to as "up selling." Another reason to add new products or services is to more evenly spread out revenues, and thereby profits, throughout the year. For example, if you are a lawn-care company that generates most profits during the spring, summer, and fall months, you may consider adding snow plowing to your complement of services in order to generate profits in what would otherwise be the off season.

CASE STUDY

It had been almost a year since EarthPower opened its doors for business. Judith had come on board four months ago as the full-time office manager and she had set up office procedures to make sure that the business was organized.

Craig spent most of his time conferencing with new customers and had just landed a large house builder out of San Francisco. The builder would include EarthPower's solar water heating units in all of its new houses in the coming year. The contract would bring in an additional $375,000 above EarthPower's original revenue estimates.

Late on a Tuesday afternoon, Craig was talking to Sun Source, one of EarthPower's solar panel suppliers. The owner of Sun Source, Jason Freed, wanted to retire and pass the business on to his son. He complained to Craig that his son had no interest in running the business and he would have to sell it to someone else.

Craig thought about the conversation long after he hung up the telephone. Sun Source provided EarthPower with almost all of its solar panels for its custom installations. If EarthPower bought out Sun Source, the profit that would otherwise be going to someone else would instead be staying in the pockets of Craig and his partner.

Craig presented the proposal at the next meeting of the board of directors. John Wendsley immediately recognized the benefits of the proposal.

"We'll be able to control the supply of panels," he said. "That will certainly help if we grow as quickly as our projections suggest for next year."

The following week, EarthPower presented its offer to Jason Freed, who accepted it after consulting with his lawyer and accountant. Jason was happy that his company was being purchased by people who had the same commitment to alternative energy as he did. Craig and his partner were happy that they were able to integrate a critical operation into their own company.

Develop a franchise

Once you have developed your business model and internal hard and soft systems, you may want to sell your business plans and systems to others who want to become small-business owners but who need guidance. If you choose this route, you would have two main revenue streams: Profits from your own business and revenues from selling franchises.

Find new markets for your existing products and services

You may find that your product or service may have wider applications than those for which you originally planned. A great example of this is the Hummer. You've probably seen one: An oversized off-road vehicle that was originally developed for military applications. The Hummer has found its way into consumer use and now bears the mark of prestige for people with enough disposable income to purchase one. Finding new markets for existing products or services can be one of the lowest cost methods of expanding your business.

Vertical Expansion

Vertical expansion refers to reaping benefits from closely related operations. For example, if you own a delicatessen, it may make sense for you to purchase the cheese-making operation that sells you your cheese. That way, you can keep the profits that would otherwise be going to the cheese maker. Another example would be if your company designs electronic circuitry for use in consumer electronics, such as stereos and DVD players. You may consider producing the consumer products yourself and selling them through your own retail outlet, and thereby harvesting the profits that the manufacturer and the retailer would normally keep.

Vertical expansion can also provide you with more control over your sources of supply.

If you control the supply chain, production scheduling becomes easier and purchasing opportunities can benefit the entire chain. The risk of vertical expansion is that you might step on the toes of your customers or suppliers. You will now be competing in their markets as well. You may find that a competitor may not be as willing to sell to you now that you are battling head to head for customers.

The Dangers of Expansion

Now that we've looked at the benefits of expanding your business, we need to look at the potential risks. Many of these risks mirror those that you faced when first starting up your business. The repercussions of business failure are greater, however, once you have established your business and have created a rapport with your customers. You have more at stake now and the risks of expansion should be carefully weighed against the potential rewards. Consider some of the risks discussed below.

Liquidity issues

Expansion usually requires additional financing to purchase equipment, hire new staff, or develop new products. This increase in debt-servicing costs (that is to say, principal and interest payments) can stretch the business's resources thin, especially in the period directly following the expansion and before the increase in revenues happens. Proper cash flow planning and forecasting can go a long way towards making sure that you don't end up on the wrong side of "stretched thin."

Triggering call provisions

When planning the financing of your expansion, be sure to review all existing debt and equity financing contracts to ensure that you will not violate any of the provisions in them. For example, your existing bank loan contract may stipulate that you have a debt to equity ratio of no more than 1:1. If your new financing causes you to go over this limit, you run the risk of your bank calling the existing loan and you may find yourself scrambling to replace it. (See Table 1 in Chapter 7 for more detail on ratios.)

If you have equity investors, either in the form of minority shareholders or venture capitalists, make sure that you fully review the voting provisions in the agreements with regards to major decisions such as expansion and mergers and acquisitions.

Increase in fixed costs

If your expansion includes new fixed costs, such as equipment lease contracts or premises rental, your business is at a greater risk of loss if the new revenue streams do not occur as planned. For example, if your expansion plan calls for $75,000 in additional revenues in the first six months following the expansion, and the actual figures are only $50,000, you still must incur all of the additional fixed costs and this can put a strain on your existing operations. Careful cash flow forecasting and a backup financing plan can soften this risk.

Calculating the Benefits of Expansion

How do you know whether expanding your business makes financial sense? The decision process is much the same as the one you followed for starting your business in the first place. When you first made the decision about whether to buy an existing business or build one from scratch, you compared all of the inflows of cash from each business to the outflows. In a comparative situation like that, you would choose the one with the largest net cash inflow using the discounted cash flow method.

In deciding whether or not to expand, we use a similar process. In this situation, we will only need to look at the *changes* in cash flows from the expansion. Any cash flows that will be the same whether or not we expand will be ignored as they will have no bearing on our decision. We will also use the discounted cash flow method but this time, our decision will be based on whether there is a net inflow or outflow of cash over a period of time. If the cash flow is positive, it makes financial sense to expand. If it is negative, it does not.

Let's look at an example:

Grace owns a market garden operation. She farms three acres and grows a variety of organic vegetables, which she sells to area restaurants as well as at the local farmer's market on Saturday mornings. She is considering expanding her business to sell to more retail customers by delivering baskets of organic vegetables to their doors on a weekly basis for 17 weeks of the year. The baskets would be a mixture of the vegetables in season that week. Grace has estimated the following:

Costs:

- She will need to till an additional acre to service her estimated 125 new customers.

- Her operating costs (seeds, labor, equipment maintenance, fertilizer) for each acre average $9,410 per season.

- She will also need to acquire a van for deliveries and hire a delivery person for 35 hours per week at $12.50 per hour. The van costs will average $0.74 per mile and she estimates the mileage per season to be approximately 3,795 miles. The lease cost for the van will be $495 per month for 48 months (four years).

Revenues:

- Grace will charge each customer $425 per season for the basket program. This will be paid at the beginning of the season.

- She is expecting 50 customers in the first year and 70, 110, and 125 customers in years two, three, and four, respectively.
- She does not feel that the new program will cut into her farmer's market revenues at all.

Because Grace's fixed costs of the new venture, namely the lease payments on the van, extend over four years, we will look at the revenues and expenses over that period of time.

Table 3 shows the cash flows. The cash flows show that in the first year of operation, there is an expected loss on the basket program. Years two to four show net cash inflows. As we have seen earlier in this book, cash today is worth more than cash tomorrow.

Therefore, early losses count for more than cash inflows later. In order to see if cash later is worth more or less than the earlier loss, we will use the discounted cash flow method to bring all of the net cash flows back to today. We will use the Present Value of $1 table in Appendix 1. Grace will have to finance the net cash outflow in year one with an operating line of credit from her bank that carries an interest rate of 12 percent, so we will use that rate for our discounting.

As you can see in Table 4, the net discounted cash flow attributed to the proposed expansion is positive, so it makes financial sense for Grace to go ahead. She will need to keep in mind that for the first season, she will have to finance the proposed cash shortfall, so this will need to be taken into account as she plans for the expansion.

TABLE 3
CASH FLOWS FOR GRACE'S MARKET GARDEN

	1	2	3	4
Revenue	21,250	29,750	46,750	53,125
Acreage	9,410	9,410	9,410	9,410
Vehicle	2,808	2,808	2,808	2,808
Lease	5,940	5,940	5,940	5,940
Delivery	7,438	7,438	7,438	7,438
Loan interest	522	-	-	-
Net cash flow	**(4,868)**	**4,154**	**21,154**	**27,529**

TABLE 4
DISCOUNTED CASH FLOWS FOR GRACE'S MARKET GARDEN

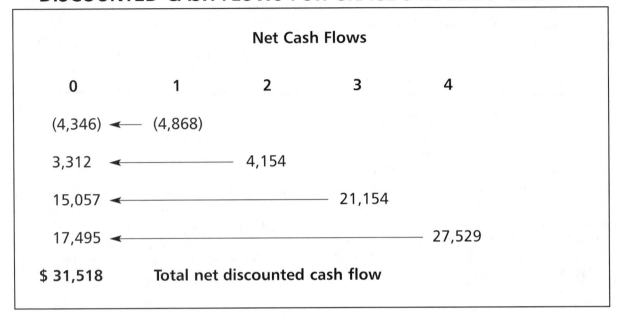

Net Cash Flows

0	1	2	3	4
(4,346) ← (4,868)				
3,312 ← 4,154				
15,057 ← 21,154				
17,495 ← 27,529				

$ 31,518   **Total net discounted cash flow**

Finding the Money to Expand

Once your business has a proven track record of financial success, your financing options begin to widen. Those who seemed reticent to lend to you when you were just starting out may be warming up to the investment possibilities as you plan your expansion.

Before you seek financing for the new operations, spend time updating your business plan, refining your cash flow forecasts, and honing your verbal presentation to potential investors or lenders. You are once again presenting yourself and your business and asking people to take a chance on you and give you money. You should be as professional as possible. You are now coming to the table as a seasoned entrepreneur, not just someone with a potentially good idea.

As you are updating your financial information, review your current financing structure. Are you getting the lowest interest rate possible on your borrowings? You may wish to refinance your current operations while you are seeking new financing. Start by talking to your bank. They may be more willing to renegotiate funding positions now that you have a track record.

Venture capitalists may also begin to show interest in your operations. Venture capitalists rarely lend money to start-ups but are more interested in the expansion of successful businesses. If your ultimate goal is to cash out of the business in five to ten years, this might be an avenue worth pursuing. For a more in-depth discussion of sources of financing, please refer to Chapters 7 and 8 regarding debt and equity financing, respectively.

Another source of financing available to you that wasn't when you first started up is internal cash flow. You may be able to divert profits from the current operations to fund the expansion in the short term. If you have significant equity investors, however, they may not be crazy about the idea of deferring the cash that should be in their pockets now for a slice of a potentially bigger pie later. It's important to make sure that all lenders and investors are on board with your plans for expansion.

Chapter Summary

➡ Planning for the expansion of your business is much like the initial planning you undertook when you started up.

➡ You can expand horizontally, increasing your revenues by introducing new products or services or new markets, or you can expand vertically, increasing revenues by taking over connected operations.

➡ You can calculate the benefits of expansion by discounting the projected cash flows.

➡ There are more avenues of funding when you expand now that you have a proven financial track record.

part
2

GROW YOUR BUSINESS

Chapter
17

The Successful Entrepreneur

Why Small Businesses Fail

As a resource to small-business owners, I've been a part of the business life of thousands of companies. I've seen entrepreneurs take the seed of an idea and turn it into a multi-million dollar enterprise with dozens of employees. But, I've also seen entrepreneurs with that same great drive and vision fail — and fail miserably. What's the difference between these two types of entrepreneurs? How can two people with the same entrepreneurial spirit have such opposite outcomes?

My experience has shown me that successful business owners understand the importance of thinking about the business holistically. They don't just focus on their great idea, but they build a business from the ground up, taking care with every part of it.

They know they need a strong foundation for their business so they can build on it. With a strong foundation, they know they can expect their business to stay standing over the years. What makes a strong foundation when it comes to building a business? Successful owners know they need to build a broad base of skills in areas such as bookkeeping, financial management, and human resources. While those may not be the "sexiest" of activities, certainly not as exciting as choosing a logo or going public, they are critical to the success of the business.

Statistics abound when it comes to small-business failure in North America. Similar statistics exist in almost every country that harbors free enterprise. Here's one that will shock you: Over ten years, 96 percent of all small businesses fail. You read that correctly. For every 100 businesses started today, only four will still be around in ten years. What a horrible toll on people's lives!

That's the bad news. Here's the good news. According to a recent Dun and Bradstreet study, more than 85 percent of business failures are preventable. How? By better management, and in particular, better financial management. Despite what many people and the media will have you believe, it's not the competition or acts of God that sink these businesses. It's a lack of management skills and a poor foundation for the business. The good news is that these skills can be learned.

Managing versus Doing

Of all the challenges that entrepreneurs face when they start a small business, I see one critical problem time and time again. Many entrepreneurs lack the ability to differentiate between managing the business and doing what the business does.

For example, if you own and manage a variety store, then preparing budgets falls into the category of "managing the business," while waiting on customers is "doing what the business does."

It's easy to get caught up in the day-to-day workings of the business. Generally, most entrepreneurs are also managers, customer service representatives, human resource managers, and sales and marketing departments — and they probably have to clean the toilets too!

This problem is common in start-up companies. A hairdresser thinks that because he can cut hair, he can run a salon. A plumber opens up a plumbing business. Someone who makes a good cup of coffee thinks she can run a coffee shop. What these business owners don't realize is that management skill is a separate ability from the skill that it takes to do what the business does.

The Four Foundation Walls

There are four key management skills that every entrepreneur needs to succeed. You can look at them as the four walls that make up the foundation of a house. As you know, you can't properly build a house on a weak or badly formed foundation. Well, you may be able to get it built, but it won't last long.

Here's what it takes to succeed, whether your business is a sidewalk lemonade stand or Microsoft:

- Entrepreneurial drive and vision
- Record keeping
- Financial management
- Planning and strategizing

Take a look at Diagram 1.

CASE STUDY

Vivian set her coffee cup down on Becky's desk. Joe and Becky had set up an appointment with her to discuss the growth plans of Joe's Plumbing.

"So what made you decide that now is the time to grow?" asked Vivian.

"Joe seems to work all the time now, and neither of us has enough time to devote to proper planning," Becky said. "We'd like to get the business to a point that it will almost run without us." She smiled at Joe. "Then maybe we can have a real vacation."

Joe chimed in. "And we've put into practice everything you've taught us. We have a real bookkeeping system now that lets us stay on top of our receivables and payables, and we know how to review our financial statements to figure out how we've done. Thanks to you, we even filed our taxes on time this year."

"You've done a great job getting a handle on your business up to this point," Vivian said. "But now, there are some things we must do before we start to grow the business. We need to have a look at the processes and procedures you have in place for your business and make sure that they are efficient and will handle the increase in business. Doing the planning upfront will save you immeasurable time down the road. Let's start with the basics."

Diagram 1
THE FOUR FOUNDATION WALLS

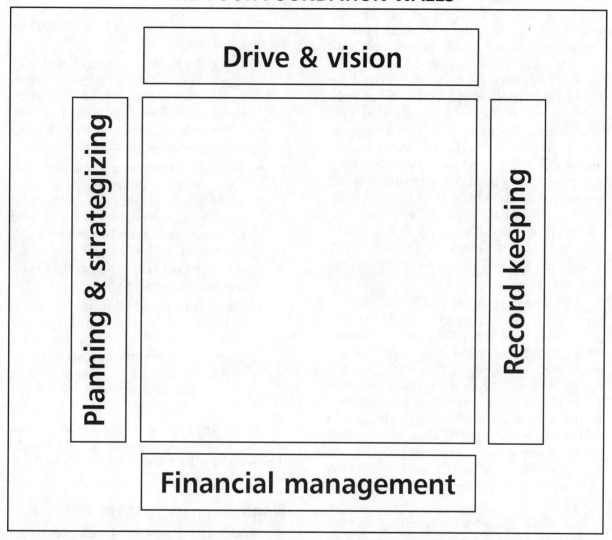

Drive & vision

Planning & strategizing

Record keeping

Financial management

Entrepreneurial drive and vision

Every business starts with someone's vision. Vision is one of the main characteristics of an entrepreneur. An entrepreneur has the drive to build a business, with an image of what that business will look like down the road. He or she has the ability to think through a situation or look at a situation and see opportunity where many others would see nothing but problems. A true entrepreneur has confidence in himself or herself and a way of thinking that is unique. A real entrepreneur is born with these characteristics. You either have them or you don't, and they are impossible to teach. Without this first foundation wall, a successful enterprise is impossible.

Record keeping

The second foundation wall is record keeping. You have to keep track of the numbers for your business. Now, this seems self-evident, but time after time, I see business owners walk through my office door with a box (or more likely several boxes) of receipts, chits, and deposit books representing six, seven, or eight years' worth of financial records that they need magically turned into financial statements and tax returns. The only reason they're finally doing this is because the government has frozen their business bank accounts. Of course, as an accountant, I can always help them get caught up and get the government off their backs, but it's no way to run a business. They have no idea if they're winning or losing, never mind if they're actually making any money.

I sit down with each of these business owners. I fix their paper trail problems and talk about the need to get a better grip on the bookkeeping and ongoing financial management of their business. Often, sadly, it's too late by then, and they're living hand-to-mouth. They spend enormous amounts of time trying to decide what payments they can bounce so that the paychecks don't. They have neither the time nor money — or, most probably, the energy — left to set up a proper operational plan and monitor it regularly.

Recording your business's numbers involves much more than just setting up software such as *QuickBooks* or *Peachtree*. These programs don't actually do the record keeping for you. You need to plan out what information you must capture to run a successful business and how to best report that information. Recording the results of your operations is a critical wall in the foundation of the house you're building. Everything else rests on it, and if you spend the time necessary to set up your bookkeeping system the right way, you've created a solid wall.

What does it take to set up a proper bookkeeping system?

- **The right tools:** Every business is different. The method you use to collect the information you need should be based on the needs of your business, whether the solution is *QuickBooks* or an *Excel* spreadsheet or a manual ledger.

- **The right information:** What information is critical to know? Do you need to know which of your ten products is making the most money? Do you need to know how many hours you billed out this month? Then you need to set up your bookkeeping system to track this information for you.

- **The right output:** How are you going to look at this information? My experience has shown me that if you make your system too time intensive or elaborate, it breaks down. You should be able to get at the results with a few clicks of the mouse.

Setting up and maintaining a proper record keeping system is covered in the first book of the *Numbers 101 for Small Business* series, *Bookkeepers' Boot Camp*.

Financial management

The third foundation wall is financial management: Understanding what the numbers are telling you. It's no use having your sales figures broken down 700 different ways if you can't tell whether or not you made money last year, or if you can't tell if one part of your operation is needlessly draining cash from the whole business.

You can't really know how you are doing and which way to go next without a basic understanding of your business numbers. Even businesses that have been around for a decade or more can struggle with this concept. Their owners and managers either can't or won't read their financial statements. So many financial disasters can be uncovered early through proper analysis. And like any disease of the body, early detection usually lowers the death rate. A wise entrepreneur can diagnose many impending business disasters and start treatment early to prevent further bleeding.

Financial management means taking all the figures you've tracked and testing them against some benchmarks. Ask yourself: Do you know what financial ratios are? If you do, are you familiar with the key financial ratios for your business? Do you have any idea what your break-even or capacity levels are? These are important markers for your business. They can tell you about profit, liquidity, and solvency. They can tell you if you have too much exposure to debt or too little. They can tell you if you have enough money in the short term and the long term.

Think of these benchmark tests as laboratory tests that a doctor would order if you weren't feeling well. Through laboratory analysis of your blood, you'd learn if your potassium levels are too high, for example. The doctor would compare your results to benchmarks in order to assess whether or not your levels are normal. Once you have learned to read your financial information, financial analysis can tell you whether your business is operating at a normal level or if there is some underlying disease. And, like many diseases of the body, it's important to catch the symptoms of your business's disease early before the situation becomes terminal.

Financial Management 101, the second book in the *Numbers 101 for Small Business* series, teaches you how to interpret the story that your numbers are telling you.

Planning and strategizing

The final foundation wall of your business is planning and strategizing, which is different from entrepreneurial vision, although it may sound similar at first. Planning and strategizing takes your business's historical performance and projects it into the future. It helps you understand the impact of both internal and external forces on your future financial performance and allows you to take steps to make any necessary changes.

For example, a business can be seemingly running along just fine, oblivious to its financial position. There always seems to be enough money in the bank to cover expenses, and the income statement that prints off almost automatically every month from the software program tells the owner that there is indeed net income. Then the business decides to have a big promotion; they will provide three hours of free technical support for every computer they sell.

They buy 600 units from their supplier, for which they have 30-day terms (i.e., they have to pay the supplier in 30 days). The promotion starts the next week and runs for two weeks. Every customer gets 30 days to pay. The problem is that the business will need to pay its supplier before the money comes in from the customers, which can lead to a serious cash flow issue. And it all could have been prevented by projecting cash needs into the future and strategizing.

In this book, we'll examine the issues of effectively planning and strategizing for your business.

Checklist 1
THE SUCCESSFUL ENTREPRENEUR

1. I have spent time mapping out the long-term direction of my business. ❏

2. I know my strengths and weaknesses as an entrepreneur. ❏

3. For those skills in which I am the weakest, I have formulated a plan to learn the necessary information. ❏

4. I have a record-keeping system for my company that gives me accurate and timely information. ❏

5. I have determined the critical revenue and expense breakdowns that will help me to manage my business strategically. ❏

6. I have calculated my break-even and capacity points for my business. ❏

7. I know what the key financial ratios are for my particular business. ❏

8. I know how to read my financial statements and understand the story they are telling me. ❏

9. I have prepared cash flow projections for my business for the next five years. ❏

10. I have carved out at least 20 percent of my time for planning and strategizing activities. ❏

Chapter Summary

➡ Most small-business failures can be prevented by learning basic financial management skills.

➡ Smart business owners spend time managing the business and not just doing what the business does.

➡ There are four critical skills that all entrepreneurs need to run a successful business: entrepreneurial drive and vision, record keeping, financial management, and planning and strategizing.

➡ Effective planning and strategizing allows the small business owner to predict challenges and opportunities in the future.

Chapter

18

The Life Cycle of a Business

It may be difficult for you to think of any business, especially your own, as having a fixed life span. You probably would like to think that your business will outlive you and your children and grandchildren — that it will still be around 500 years from now. But, in reality, that is not likely.

It's almost impossible to determine how long your business will last. Some companies have survived generations, although these too will someday cease to exist. Japan's Hoshi Hotel has been around since 718 AD, surviving almost 50 generations of the Hoshi family. Barovier & Toso has been making glass in Venice since 1295. The oldest existing family firm in the United Kingdom, John Brooke & Sons, Ltd., has been in operation since 1541. In North America, the Hudson's Bay Company first started fur trading in 1670. Each of these companies has experienced ups and downs over their long and venerable existence, but they have still followed the same life cycle that your business will experience.

The Three Stages of a Business

Every business goes through a natural evolution over its lifetime. The only difference between businesses is how quickly they progress through the cycles.

The natural life cycle of any business can be broken into three stages: infancy, maturity, and decline (see Diagram 2). Each of the stages has unique identifiers. A business in the infancy stage, for example, will have operational characteristics and trends that are very different from a business in the decline stage.

Let's look at each stage in more detail.

Infancy

Infancy is where every new business starts out. It is a time signified by negative cash flows, rapid growth, and capacity bottlenecks.

Businesses that are just beginning their operations often find that their outflows of cash

Diagram 2
THE LIFE CYCLE OF A BUSINESS

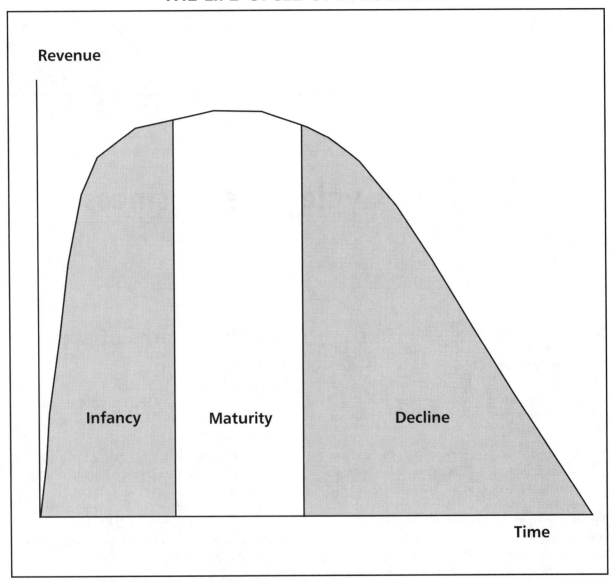

are greater than their inflows. If you start your business from scratch, you must build up your customer base before you have revenue. However, fixed expenses like rent, office staff, and insurance have to be paid whether you have no customers or 1,000 customers. The negative

cash flow this creates is usually temporarily fixed by either owner investment or bank financing.

In general, businesses that are very capital intensive (e.g., those that require significant specialized equipment) have a greater negative cash flow at the beginning of their life cycle. Once revenues are high enough to cover both the direct cost of the product or service being sold and the overhead costs, then they begin to make profits. (For a fuller discussion of fixed cost behavior, refer the second book of the *Numbers 101 for Small Business* series, *Financial Management 101*.)

Businesses in the start-up phase tend to have quite dramatic revenue growth, which is easy to understand when you consider that when you grow from having no customers to one customer, you have increased revenues by 100 percent! If the business is filling a market niche, customers will either come over from other suppliers or will realize the need for the product or service, perhaps for the first time. Your customer base will continue to grow until the market need has been filled (i.e., all the potential customers have already come over). At this point, your business begins to move into the maturity phase.

Another frequent characteristic of infancy is that the business regularly hits its capacity. For example, a manufacturer will run his or her current equipment to its maximum capacity before he or she purchases a new one. A service provider will have his or her staff working overtime before hiring new staff.

Most of the consideration here is financial and relates back to the negative cash flows that we talked about earlier. If you don't have the money for new equipment, you will nurse your old equipment along for as long as you can. Another reason that capacity is often reached, though, relates to the ability (or inability) of the new entrepreneur to accurately predict demand for the product or service. If that demand and its related sales are underestimated, a business can be left scrambling to get orders filled quickly. Once a business has a longer history, and its manager has a better understanding of the industry and its trends, capacity issues become less pronounced.

When a business better understands its markets and customers and has absorbed most of the excess market demand in its industry, it will begin to shift into the maturity stage.

Maturity

In the maturity phase, a business has found its place in its industry and can more accurately predict its revenues and expenses.

The maturity phase is denoted by stable revenue growth (perhaps 5 percent to 10 percent per year) and positive cash flows. Mature businesses provide a consistent return to their investors and a stable salary to their managers.

Businesses stay in the maturity phase until they begin to decline, either through obsolescence or changes in the external market.

It is in the maturity phase that a business must begin to plan for its own demise (much like an individual should engage in retirement and estate planning well before those events take place).

Decline

Every business eventually begins to slow down. Revenues begin to taper off and cash flow once again becomes a problem.

Why do once-healthy businesses die? Frequently, it's because the services or products that the business sells are no longer needed in the market place. Consumer tastes change or technology has advanced so that new products take the place of old ones. Forward-thinking businesses can stave off this decline, at least in the short term, by changing with the times and offering new products or services. Eventually, however, new players will enter the field and will erode market share.

Businesses have differing responses to going into the "golden years" of their existence. If a business is not planning and strategizing appropriately, it may not even realize it is in decline. The business can struggle along for several years in this phase (at least until the money runs out) and not understand why revenues are declining and cash flow is tight.

Other businesses put themselves up for sale, realizing that they still have solid components that a newer business may want to integrate into their operations. Some businesses choose to wind up operations and the investors find other avenues of investment.

At What Stage of the Life Cycle Is Your Business?

By using the signposts and discussion above, you should be able to figure out where your business fits into the life cycle model. Is it a new business, with leaping revenues and no cash? Or is it more stable, with a predictable market demand?

It's important to know at what stage your business is in its life cycle, because it will help you in a myriad of ways, especially in the planning and strategizing area.

A real-life example of a company that understood its own vulnerability to obsolescence is the Minnesota Mining & Manufacturing Company. The name of this company may not be familiar to you but I'm sure you have heard of 3M, which is the name the company adopted as they changed their products over the years.

3M was born in 1902 in Two Harbors, Minnesota. Five investors started the company in order to mine a mineral deposit for grinding-wheel abrasives. This didn't work out because the deposit was found to have little value. The company began to focus on sandpaper products. Business was difficult in the start-up years and the company struggled until it could find more investors and develop new products.

In 1925, one of the laboratory assistants invented masking tape and a whole new line of products was born. 3M created Scotch tape, Scotchlite Reflective Sheeting for highway markings, and magnetic sound-recording tape. They invented dozens of products that we now would have a difficult time living without, including some that were originally intended for wartime use. In the 1970s and 1980s, 3M expanded into pharmaceuticals, radiology, energy control, and the office market (Post-It Notes being the major invention in this area).

3M is now a multinational corporation with revenues of over US $15 billion a year. The company reports that approximately 30 percent of these sales come from products created in the past four years. 3M understood that its strength was creating new products for emerging markets using its core technologies. Had this company stuck to its original mandate of mining or even of selling sandpaper, it would not be around today. 3M has not hit decline yet as it has always managed to adapt to current market conditions. You must also do this in your small business if it is to survive.

How Can My Business Use This Information?

Knowing your business's place in the life cycle indicates a lot about what to expect in the coming years.

For example, if you have been in business for three years and have had revenue growth of 92 percent the first year, 76 percent the second year, and 14 percent the third year, you may be entering the maturity phase. Therefore, it would be ridiculous to predict 75 percent revenue growth in the fourth year. As Diagram 2 shows, in the maturity phase, revenue growth begins to slow as it climbs towards the top of the arch. It would probably make more sense to predict 8 percent to 10 percent growth in the fourth year.

If you have noticed a decline in revenues, triggering a more problematic cash flow, your business may be starting to decline. It's important to examine the underlying causes of the decline. Are there new products on the market? Do you have a customer service issue (i.e., can someone else do what you do faster, with better guarantees or fewer hassles)? You can only devise a response to the decline if you understand the cause.

Checklist 2
THE LIFE CYCLE OF A BUSINESS

1. I know which life cycle stage my business is in. ☐

2. I have projected my business's growth rate using the life cycle information. ☐

3. I have planned how to prolong the maturity phase of my business. ☐

4. I have analyzed the demand for my business's product or service and am comfortable that I can meet my customers' expectations. ☐

5. I have analyzed the external market conditions that affect my business and I understand the trends that will impact my business's future revenues. ☐

6. I have considered new products or services that I can offer in order to continue my company's growth. ☐

7. I have reviewed the opportunities to purchase and integrate another business into my own to strengthen market demand. ☐

Chapter Summary

➡ Even the most successful businesses have fixed lives.

➡ The life cycle of every business can be broken into three stages: infancy, maturity, and decline.

➡ It's important to know where your business fits into the life cycle so that you can plan and strategize effectively.

➡ You can respond in a variety of ways to a declining business. It is therefore imperative to recognize and understand when your business is in this stage.

Chapter

19

A Systems Approach

What would you say if I told you that your small business has a lot in common with McDonald's or FedEx? You may wonder at first what, if anything, your small business has to do with these franchises. They are giants in their respective industries and employ thousands of people. Your business, on the other hand, is made up of you and perhaps a handful of staff.

But these large franchises were once small, too. They started with one person's dream of how a business should operate. Those entrepreneurs experimented with their business models time and time again until they got it right.

What successful franchises have done exceedingly well is to build and monitor systems in their procedures.

At McDonald's, for example, there is a system for greeting the customer, a system for preparing the food, and a system for cleaning the bathrooms. These and a myriad of other

systems allow you, the customer, to have a consistent experience every time you visit. Neither the president of McDonald's nor the restaurant manager needs to be there to make sure you're properly looked after.

Are you able to say the same thing about your business? Or do you feel that you need to be there every minute to make sure that nothing disastrous happens?

Let's take a look at how franchises work and the systems they use. Then we can begin designing your business to operate in a similarly effective manner.

Anatomy of a Franchise

You may not consciously think about this when you walk into your favorite Dunkin' Donuts to pick up your daily honey dip or when you pull into Midas Muffler to get your seasonal lube, oil, and filter, but from the moment you enter the door, you have witnessed a process. If you walk into these businesses tomorrow or the day after that, you will have a practically identical experience. And that is the strength of a franchise. Customers know exactly what to expect. They know that they will be greeted in the same manner, that the product or service will be the same quality every time, and any customer issue will be handled in the same way.

A Real-Life Example

Let's have a look at a real franchise. Geeks On Call® is a company that provides on-site computer services to residential and commercial customers. Geeks is a franchise. The head office sells the exclusive rights to franchisees to operate in a certain territory. It also provides ongoing support and assistance to the franchisees to help them operate their businesses in a consistent and profitable manner according to the Geeks strategy.

To become a Geeks franchisee, you must pay a franchise fee upfront, and then ongoing fees, to the head office for advertising. You also pay them a royalty of a certain percentage of your sales. In return, you reap the benefits of the Geeks advertising campaigns and ongoing technical and sales support.

Do you have to be a computer programmer to run a Geeks franchise? Absolutely not (although many are). The main criteria are entrepreneurial drive and vision. You can hire the computer technicians to work for you. This is the benefit of a systems approach — the systems and expertise have already been developed and, as long as you follow the systems, you will be a successful business owner. It's the same reason that you do not need to be a chef (or even be able to boil water) to become a McDonald's franchisee.

Benefits of a Systems Approach

The benefits of taking what franchises do well and applying those concepts to your own business are many. How would you feel if every time you walked into your favorite Dunkin' Donuts, the experience was different? Now put yourself in your customers' shoes. Do you want them to have the same comfort level when dealing with you, always knowing what to expect? Of course you do! It will not only set you apart from your competitors in your customers' eyes, but it will also make the operation of the business much more effective and enjoyable for you.

CASE STUDY

"One of the reasons you both are feeling so overwhelmed," Vivian said, "is that you both *are* the business."

Joe looked puzzled. "I'm not sure what you mean by that. Of course, we are the business. There's no one else."

Vivian smiled. "But there will never be anyone else until you begin to systematize your business."

"Oh, I think I understand," Becky said. "You mean we have to write down how we do things, kind of like an operations manual."

"Well, I do mean that," Vivian said, "but it's more than that too. You need to start looking at your business and personal goals to make sure that your growth plan will fit in with them. Then you will have to make sure that each of your processes and procedures gets you to your goal. If you just start growing without doing this legwork first, it's like turning on a fire hose full blast without controlling the stream of water. It will be all over the place."

Joe frowned. "And then we'd be working even more."

Another often-overlooked benefit of taking a systems approach to your business is that, when you are ready to sell your business, you will have created a much more valuable business and will generally receive a higher price. Why is that? Think about it from the buyer's perspective. The buyer is purchasing a business that is practically "turnkey," meaning that they can walk in and, from day one, run the business exactly the same way that you did. They are buying the systems: The procedures and operations manuals that will ensure that they will be as successful as you have been.

Your Business as a Machine

Looking at your business as if it were a machine with cogs and wheels may be a new perspective for you. The more you see your business as a tangible thing, however, the more you will be able to envision what needs to be done to make it as effective and efficient as possible. You will need to make the fundamental paradigm shift from "I make money for myself" to "my business makes money for me." Although that may seem like a small change in wording, it represents a huge change in thinking — one that will make your business successful.

Becoming the Head Mechanic

Once you have made the shift to "my business makes money for me," your role in the business becomes clearer. Your main role is not to do what the business does (e.g., make bagels, cut hair, design buildings), although you may still function in that capacity. Your main role is to increase the operating efficiency of the business machine. You will ensure that all employees are following the systems that you have put in place and are performing consistently.

Becoming the head mechanic means that you will not be buried in the minutia of the business for 12 hours a day, but will truly be in a management role, helping your employees to be a part of the machine.

As head mechanic, your main tasks will be —

- Ensuring compliance with the systems
- Reviewing the impact the systems are having on the financial health of the business
- Constantly testing the effectiveness of existing systems and altering them as required
- Building new systems as the business grows

Once you understand your true role in your business, you will find that you spend less time managing and have created more time for planning and strategizing.

Checklist 3
A SYSTEMS APPROACH

1   I have considered the benefits of systematizing my business. ☐

2.   I have taken notice of franchises that I deal with frequently and understand their systems. ☐

3.   I understand that my main function in my business is to manage and grow it; not just work in it. ☐

4.   I have mapped out my major management functions in my business. ☐

5.   I have analyzed my business from my customers' perspective. ☐

6.   I have put a plan in place that allows me to spend at least 20 percent of my time on planning and strategizing activities. ☐

Chapter Summary

➡ Businesses of all sizes can learn from what franchises do best, which is building and monitoring systems.

➡ Having systems in place in your business allows you as the owner/manager to provide your customers with a more consistent buying experience. This keeps them coming back.

➡ Having "turnkey" systems in place allows you to reap more wealth when you sell the business.

➡ Once you become your business's "head mechanic," you will create more time to plan and strategize.

Chapter
20

Analyzing the Status Quo

Before we can look at growing your business soundly, we need to make sure that the foundation walls of your business's house have been solidly built. In Chapter 17, we looked at the four foundation walls of your business:

- Entrepreneurial drive and vision
- Record keeping
- Financial management
- Planning and strategizing

Let's take a more detailed look at each of these areas and make sure that your business is sound.

Entrepreneurial Drive and Vision

This is all about you and the vision that you have for your business. Remember back to when your business was nothing but an insistent

thought in your head. You may have been working for someone else or raising your children or finishing school, but you knew what you wanted to do and how it should look.

That vision and drive to create a business should still be there now. In other words, the first criterion for *growing* a business successfully is the same as for *starting* one: The force of will and the creativity to create something spectacular.

Take some time and make sure that the spark is still there. If, for example, you currently feel burned out and overwhelmed by the day-to-day operations of the business, you will need some time to regenerate yourself before you can put your efforts and talents into growing your business. Once you have made sure that your fundamental drive is still there, then it's time to examine the other three foundation walls.

Record Keeping

Okay, discussing bookkeeping is not the most exciting thing in the world, but, as you know by now, it is critical.

Examine your record keeping practices. Here's a quick checklist for you:

- Is your bookkeeping up to date?

- Are all supplier payments and government remittances being paid on time?

- Is your bookkeeping system giving you the information you need on a timely basis?

- Has your business outgrown your bookkeeping system?

- Are you doing your own bookkeeping when your time and talent would be better spent on managing or growing your business?

If you need a refresher on bookkeeping systems or hiring a bookkeeper, you may wish to refer back to the first book in the *Numbers 101 for Small Business* series, *Bookkeepers' Boot Camp*.

Financial Management

Once you have determined that your record keeping system is still optimal for your business, it's time to look at your financial management practices:

- Do you have an adequate system for preparing and analyzing budgets?

- Are you actively managing your business's key performance indicators?

- Do you have systems in place to track your accounts receivable and accounts payable?

- Do you have a handle on all the risks associated with your business, such as debt exposure, economic dependence, and foreign exchange risk?

If you need a refresher on financial management for your business, you may wish to

---

CASE STUDY

"Tell me all the steps you go through when you invoice a customer," Vivian said, her pencil poised above her notebook.

"Well," said Becky, chewing on her bottom lip, "that's hard because I probably don't do it the same way every time."

"Just outline your usual method. Say I'm a new customer and I've just had you out to rough in the plumbing for my new bathroom. What would happen next?"

"Joe would probably have you sign the work order when he was there so that we know you agree that the work was completed properly. He would bring the work order to the office and leave it on my desk. That is, if he doesn't stuff it in his jacket pocket. If he does that, I might not see it for weeks!"

"Very funny, Becky," Joe said as he rifled through his jacket pockets.

"Once I've seen the work order, I'd invoice you in the accounting system. Joe would check over the bill to make sure I hadn't forgotten anything and then I would mail it to you. Whew," she said, rubbing her forehead. "I remembered all the steps."

"Not quite finished yet, Becky. Tell me what happens after that. I know your payment terms are net 30 days, so what happens if you haven't seen a check from me by then?"

Becky chewed on her lip again and outlined the rest of the billing process for Vivian.

---

refer to the second book in the *Numbers 101 for Small Business* series, *Financial Management 101*.

Planning and Strategizing

This is the foundation wall that we will spend the most time discussing in the remainder of this book. Planning and strategizing requires taking all our knowledge of our business's historical performance and projecting it into the future. It encompasses revenue and customer base growth, as well as resource and materials planning. It involves asking questions such as: How much capital will we need 12 months from now? How many people will we be hiring? If we spend $4,000 on advertising, what will that do to revenues?

The Busy Entrepreneur

As both the owner and manager (and perhaps salesperson, office clerk, bookkeeper, and toilet cleaner) of your business, the demands on your time are many. You may feel unsure how to appropriately apportion your time. It is natural for you to spend your time on the more immediate concerns, such as bookkeeping, talking to customers, and sales, rather than planning and strategizing. A typical split of an owner/manager's time might look like Diagram 3.

As you can see, this entrepreneur only spends whatever time he or she feels is left over for planning and strategizing. Because the more immediate work tends to expand to fill available time, there is frequently no time left over for proper planning.

A more appropriate split of time is shown in Diagram 4.

As you can see, this entrepreneur has freed up much of the time he or she formerly spent on operational and management duties, and spends most of the time now on growing

Diagram 3
TYPICAL TIME CHART FOR A BUSINESS OWNER

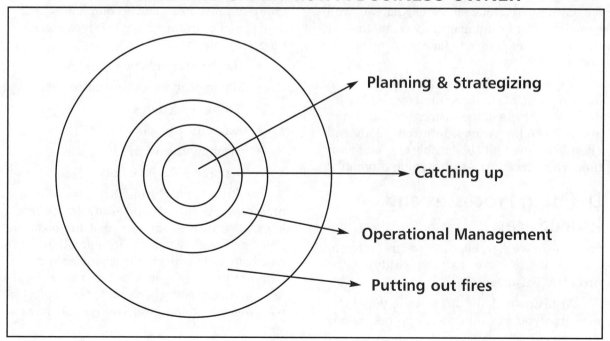

Diagram 4
RECOMMENDED TIME CHART FOR A BUSINESS OWNER

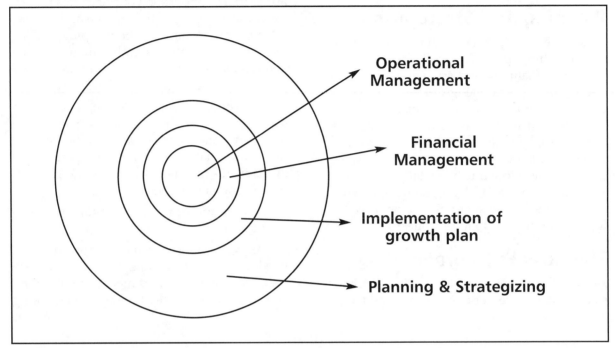

Operational Management

Financial Management

Implementation of growth plan

Planning & Strategizing

the business. You may say, "Well, that's all well and good, but I can't magically create time or hire a bunch of people to take over my operational duties."

The answer is systems. Once you have systems in place, the time required for the day-to-day management of the business will decrease. You will run the business more efficiently and effectively. You will also be able to spend your time where it counts — on growing profitably!

Defining Processes and Procedures

So, how do we start building systems into our growth model? We start by studying the processes we already have in place.

Write down all the processes in your business that you can think of. A process is any

group of procedures that accomplishes a business goal. For example, some typical business processes might be:

- Handling telephone inquiries
- Making service calls to customers
- Billing procedures
- Accounts payable
- Cleaning the office
- Managing the inventory

You'll notice right off that some of these processes are internal and some are external. Internal processes are ones that the business must perform as part of its operations, but which are not visible to the customer or client. External processes are those that directly affect the customer or client. So, for example, the way the telephone is answered can have a direct impact on whether someone becomes a new customer, whereas how the bathrooms are cleaned does not have such a direct link (although dirty bathrooms ultimately can influence a customer's decision to go elsewhere).

Once you have identified as many processes as possible, take each one and break it down into its component procedures. For example, let's start with handling telephone inquiries. A breakdown of individual procedures might look like this:

Handling telephone inquiries

1. Telephone is answered by whomever is available (Employee #1).

2. Caller is greeted pleasantly using the company name.

3. Inquiry is answered if Employee #1 knows the answer, otherwise takes a message.

4. If message taken, it is written on a piece of paper and put on the desk of the person that the employee thinks can most likely answer the question (Employee #2).

5. Message is handled by Employee #2 if he or she knows the answer, otherwise, message paper is passed to another employee (Employee #3).

These procedures make up the process of handling telephone inquiries. Now take each process in your business and document these procedures. Processes that you have forgotten will most likely present themselves to you at this time and you can add them to the list.

Note that we do not want to begin fleshing out the documentation for these processes at this time. We will be fine-tuning and in some cases getting rid of inefficient procedures and processes in the following chapters. Only once we have our new set of processes will we begin creating documentation for the processes in the form of a systems manual.

Checklist 4
ANALYZING THE STATUS QUO

1. I have re-examined my original intentions for starting my business. ☐

2. My bookkeeping is up to date and accurate. ☐

3. I have re-evaluated whether or not I need to hire a bookkeeper. ☐

4. I have an up-to-date budget for the current fiscal year. ☐

5. I have set up a management operating plan and am tracking my key financial indicators regularly. ☐

6. I have outlined all of my business's current processes for both internal and external functions. ☐

7. I have broken down all of my business processes into their individual procedures. ☐

Chapter Summary

➡ Before you can grow your business profitably, it's critical to ensure that you have your four foundation walls in place: entrepreneurial drive and vision still intact, an appropriate record keeping system, ongoing financial management, and preliminary planning and strategizing.

➡ Most of your time is probably spent on the operational side of your business, but once you have systems in place, more time will be freed up for planning and strategizing.

➡ Start the business growth process with documenting your current processes and procedures.

Chapter

21

Growing Your Business

In this chapter, we will begin to look at how to profitably grow your business. Many small businesses look only at getting new people in the door when they think about growing their business. In trying to attract these new customers, they take the "splatter gun" approach: Placing ads and running marketing campaigns based on "gut feel" and pricing. They have no idea if these programs are working or if they are sending good money down the sinkhole.

Growing your business takes more planning, testing, and discipline than that, however. In order to create a proper plan for growth, you must start by looking at what your goals are for your business.

Your Business Goals

When you first started your business, what did you envision five or ten years down the road? A huge corporation with dozens or perhaps hundreds of employees, and you sitting in the glass-walled corner office with its own fireplace and bar? Or did you have something smaller in mind, just you and a desk in your basement with the ability to run upstairs and put in a load of laundry occasionally?

Regardless of what stage your business is at, if you're contemplating growth, it's time to revisit your goals, both business and personal.

Many of these goals will be outlined in your business plan, which should be a living, breathing embodiment of your business and its projected future. (What, you don't have a business plan? Go and sit in the corner! Better yet, go back and read the second book in the *Numbers 101 for Small Business* series, *Financial Management 101*, for a discussion of financial measures and tracking systems.)

You may find that some of your goals conflict with one another. For example, you may want to pursue aggressive growth, which may entail lots of hands-on time. That will cause some challenges if another of your business goals is to spend more time with your family.

Let's take a look at some typical goals many entrepreneurs have, as well as some things for you to think about as you decide which business and personal goals are important to you.

Profit

The most common of small business goals is making money. How can you determine how much profit is reasonable to plan for? Start by looking at other businesses in your industry. It may be difficult to determine exactly what their profit position is (they're most likely private companies with confidential financial information), but with some experience you should be able to make a reasonable guess.

Start with what you know about their expenses. You should have a good handle by now on your own expenses and will therefore be able to ascertain what your competitors' cost structures must look like. Then, try to get a handle on their revenues. How many customers would you estimate they have? What does their pricing structure look like? These will provide a rough estimate of their profit. If those businesses have been in business longer than you have and are mature businesses, that level of profit is most likely reasonably attainable for your business as well.

Next, start thinking about your own profit goals. What do you need in the way of an ongoing income, either as a manager's salary or an investor's return on investment, to cover your living expenses and live comfortably? What do you want to put away into savings? Do you want to sell the business and retire early? This is where your personal and business financial goals merge. For example, if you are running a part-time T-shirt-making business out of your garage and your personal

---

CASE STUDY

Vivian punched numbers into the calculator while Joe and Becky looked over her shoulder.

"What I've heard you both say," she said, "is that you want to grow this business over the next ten years, while you both gradually want to work less on the operational side and more on the management side."

"That's right," Joe said. "And we want to be able to sell it for a million dollars in ten years and move to Tahiti." He laughed and punched Becky lightly on the arm. "Right?"

Becky looked worried. "Is that even possible, Vivian?"

"I was just joking around," said Joe. "I'll be happy to break even in ten years and maybe have our house paid for."

"If that's really true, Joe," Vivian said, "you and Becky are not going to have a very comfortable retirement. You'll be working long after you sell the business just to pay the bills. It's important to plan the growth necessary in your business to retire the way you want. I want to show you something."

Joe and Becky crowded around Vivian. "If you want the business to be worth a million dollars in ten years, you would need to grow your revenues by just under 18 percent per year, assuming that you can sell the business for one times revenues."

"You're kidding me!" Joe said, his mouth hanging open. "You mean it's actually possible?"

"Not only possible, but quite doable," Vivian said.

Becky said, "That sounds like a heck of a lot of advertising."

"Let's go over the three ways to grow Joe's Plumbing and how we can use all three of them together," Vivian said.

---

wealth goal is to become a millionaire by the age of 40, you may have to rethink one of those priorities.

Freedom

Freedom is another common entrepreneurial goal: freedom from financial worry, freedom from bosses, freedom to set your own hours, freedom to write your own destiny. There are many types of freedoms you may think about when first starting your business. The tragedy is that many small-business owners don't plan effectively enough to ever experience those freedoms. They end up chained to their businesses, chasing after the first goal: Profit.

Think about what's really important to you in the way of work-family balance. Do you want to work 20 or 60 hours per week? Do you want to be able to arrange your own work hours and not be chained to a retail location? Do you want to work as hard as possible for the first five years to get the business off the ground and then slow down? These are some important considerations when starting to develop your growth plan.

Recognition

Some entrepreneurs want to be recognized and respected — in their communities, in their industries, in their fields of expertise. You may want to be known as the leading expert in oriental rug cleaning, and your rug cleaning business is your platform from which to showcase that expertise. Take some time to consider if recognition is important to you.

Peace of mind

It may comfort you to know that you do not have to rely on anyone else for your source of income. You are creating your own wealth. This removes some of the risk that employees have of being completely dependent on an employer to get a paycheck. If this goal is important to you, it will be critical as you plan your business's growth to make sure that you recognize the more hidden sources of risk in a small business, and that you take steps to avoid them.

Planning for Growth

Now that you've looked at those business and personal goals that are important to you, it's time to begin your growth plan.

Some of this plan should already be embedded in your overall business plan. At the very least, you should have a 12-month and 5-year revenue and cash flow projection. You may also have a marketing and promotion strategy. What we are going to do now is to take that high-level planning and bring it down to street level, planning it piece by piece, testing its effectiveness, and putting numbers to it.

The revenue growth projection in your business plan may look something like this:

Year:	Revenue:	Growth:
2008	$175,000	
2009	$218,750	25%
2010	$262,500	20%
2011	$301,875	15%
2012	$332,063	10%

This growth pattern would be typical of a business that will move from the infancy stage to the maturity stage in its life cycle during this five-year period. (See Chapter 18 for a discussion of a business's life cycle.)

We need to plan exactly how to achieve those levels of revenues. It's not enough to simply place some newspaper ads and cross our fingers. We must have a step-by-step strategy. But first, let's make sure we understand the difference between good growth and bad growth.

Good versus Bad Growth

Growth is growth, you say? Take it and run! This strategy has bankrupted many small businesses. It's critical to understand why and to be able to divert yourself from that path if you find yourself starting to meander down it.

It is quite possible (and highly undesirable) to get many new customers in the door and increase revenues substantially without increasing the bottom line. How? One way is to advertise that your business has the lowest prices. In general, competing with other businesses in your industry on the basis of price is a recipe for disaster. There will always be someone new coming into the arena that is able to undercut you, and you will find yourself with ever-shrinking margins and an ever-heightening battle for new customers.

Another way to lose money when your business grows is by attracting the wrong type of customers; those who need a lot of hand-holding will call you a million times for free support and advice and will waste your time in a myriad of other ways. This is time that you could have been spending giving great service to your good customers or attracting new ones.

So, when we talk about growing your business, we only want to look at *profitable* growth; growth that contributes not only to revenues, but also to the bottom line.

The Three Ways to Grow Your Business

Take a few minutes and write down all the strategies you can think of for growing your business, from advertising to networking to word-of-mouth. Anything you can think of.

_____

_____

_____

_____

_____

_____

_____

_____

_____

_____

_____

_____

_____

_____

Now review your list.

Each of these strategies will fit into one of the three ways to grow your business that we will discuss in the remainder of this chapter.

The three ways to grow your business are by:

- Attracting new customers
- Selling them more
- Selling to them more often

That's it! It's not rocket science or any well-guarded management secret. All growth comes from doing one or a combination of those three things.

Let's look at each one in more detail.

Attracting new customers

If you take your list of strategies and group them by the above three ways of growing your business, you will most likely find that most of your strategies fall under the category of attracting new customers. Most small businesses focus on getting new people in the door. All the advertising you do supports this strategy; you are marketing to attract new people to try your product or service and, hopefully, to like it enough to come back again.

There are a number of reasons why focusing only on this strategy is dangerous:

- **It's expensive to market to new customers.** Your advertising budget is going to newspaper ads, telephone directory displays, and radio or television spots. It will probably cost you between 3 percent and 5 percent of your total expense budget to advertise to get new people in.

- **New customers are not yet loyal to you.** They really know nothing about you at this point. Think about a new store or service business that you have gone into lately. When you enter, you "feel out" how they do things and how they will treat you as a customer. You're willing to give them the opportunity to delight you but you are not yet willing to buy their product or service to the exclusion of all others. That's how new customers feel about you. They are taking a leap of faith to buy from you. You could spend all that money attracting them, but then some off-the-cuff remark from one of your staff could drive them back out the door.

- **It's difficult to bring new products and services to a cold market.** It takes time to build relationships with customers. Those who have known you and your business practices for a long time will be more receptive to you providing untraditional wares, but those who are new to you might be more wary and less likely to purchase anything they consider "strange."

Although it's important for every business to be able to attract new customers, smart businesses simultaneously focus on the customers they already have. These are the customers who have purchased from you before, know what you have to offer, and like it. They know you, your business practices, and your premises. Buying from you is comfortable and familiar to them. Why not ensure that you are getting the most from these customers? The last two methods of growing your business focus on these existing customers.

Selling them more

Another way to grow your business is to sell more to your existing customer base. This is also known as "up selling" and is an important part of the growth plans of companies such as McDonald's ("Would you like fries with that?") and amazon.com ("If you liked that, you'll love this").

Your current customer base knows you and likes what you have to offer. Chances are, they will like more of what you have to offer if you provide them with opportunities to buy more.

The benefits of working on this aspect of growth are:

- **Your existing customers are "warm."** They are already comfortable with the way you do business.

- **Offering more products or services to your customers will be perceived as "full service."** Customers like making multiple purchases at fewer places. It saves them time and energy in seeking out new businesses to meet their needs.

- **It's much less expensive to sell to current customers.** It can be done with the way you speak to them or with in-store displays rather than through expensive advertisements.

Selling to them more often

This strategy focuses on getting your customers to come back and buy more frequently. This may entail reminding customers of the range of products or services you provide. For example, if you are furnace repair company, remind your customers that you not only repair broken furnaces, but also provide a fall maintenance package to ensure that their furnaces are in good running condition for the upcoming winter. Give them more reasons to come back and see you.

Leverage Revisited

The leverage that we are talking about here is not the leverage that you associate with borrowing money. This is the leverage that you achieve by focusing on all three growth strategies at the same time: attracting new customers, selling them more every time they come in your door, and selling to them more often. Instead of scrambling to meet unreasonable growth expectations in the number of new customers you are planning for, you are better off making small incremental changes in each of the three growth areas, which is usually more realistic as well. Once you have an understanding of the numbers behind the strategy, you have the power to create immense change in your business.

Let's have a look at an example to see how this works.

Jason Forwell owns a small office-supplies shop. His revenues have been growing steadily over the past five years, but he is on the verge of expanding the premises into the vacant space next to his shop and he wants to grow his revenues quickly to be able to cover the costs of the move. Currently, he has approximately 275 regular customers. With the help of his accountant, he has determined that those customers come into the shop on average twice per year and they spend $125 every time they come in.

Therefore, Jason's revenues are —

275 customers X $125 every visit
X 2 visits = $68,750

Jason's initial plan was to advertise heavily in the local newspaper and run radio ads on the talk radio station to bring in more customers. His goal was to increase his customer base by 25 percent. This would give him revenues of —

344 customers X $125 every visit
X 2 visits = $86,000

This would represent an increase in revenue exactly equal to the increase in the customer base, or 25 percent. Jason felt that this would be enough to justify the expansion, although he was unsure as to whether it was actually possible to increase revenues by such a large percentage by advertising alone.

Jason spoke with his accountant about the plan and the accountant showed Jason that by making small changes in all three growth areas, he could have a much greater impact on revenues. Together, they mapped out the following plan:

1. Increase the customer base by 10 percent from 275 to 303. This would be accomplished through a mail-out to current customers, offering them a 10 percent discount on their next order if they bring in a new customer.

2. Increase the amount the customers spend every time they come in by 10 percent from $125 to $138. This will be accomplished through a combination

of visual displays and staff script. Commonly used items such as pens, labels, and envelopes will be prominently displayed beside the cash register. Jason will prepare a training document for the shop staff pairing common items together. For example, customers purchasing printer toner cartridges may also need copy paper; customers purchasing customized letterhead may also need business cards.

3. Jason will increase the average number of times his customers come into his shop from two to three. He will do this by surveying his customers to find out what types of goods they currently have to go to other stores to buy. For example, if Jason's shop doesn't sell office equipment, like photocopiers and printers, customers may go to a larger office supply store for those types of items. While they are there, they might also pick up some paper, computer disks, and highlighters — things that Jason does sell. Jason will find out from the surveys what he needs to stock to ensure that he keeps his customers coming back to him.

If Jason is successful in making these small incremental changes in all three of the growth strategies, this will be the impact on revenues:

**303 customers X $138 per visit
X 3 visits = $125,442**

This represents an 82 percent increase in revenues versus the 25 percent envisioned under Jason's original strategy. It's also important to note that this type of comprehensive strategy is generally less costly and more effective to implement than advertising alone.

Now that we have had a look at the three ways to grow your business and the impact of leveraging those three ways, in the next chapter we will examine in detail how to set up your business machine to grow profitably.

Checklist 5
GROWING YOUR BUSINESS

1. I have prepared a business plan for my company. ☐

2. I have reviewed my profit goals to ensure they are compatible with other companies in my industry. ☐

3. I have assessed my personal need for a balance between work and family life. ☐

4. I have assessed my own risk tolerance in growing and managing my business. ☐

5. I have prepared a 12-month and 5-year revenue projection. ☐

6. I have outlined several growth strategies and have categorized them between attracting new customers, selling them more, and selling to them more often. ☐

7. I have prepared a growth plan for my business that leverages all three growth methods. ☐

Chapter Summary

➡ Before you put any growth plan in place for your business, it's important to review both your personal and business goals to ensure that the plans will integrate with each other.

➡ Growth for growth's sake is not a great business creed. It's important to seek out only profitable growth.

➡ Although there are many strategies to grow your business, they can all be grouped into only three overall methods: attracting new customers, selling them more every time they come through the door, and getting them to come through the door more often.

➡ Concentrating on all three methods simultaneously and making small incremental changes in all three will provide you with great leverage to increase your revenues.

Getting a Handle on Your Revenues

Before we can start positioning your business for profitable growth, it's important to get a handle on where your business is at right now. In Chapter 20, we looked at your current processes and procedures to get a preliminary look at the "inner workings" of your business.

In this chapter, we want to look at your revenue streams. You may not have thought about what your historical revenues can predict for the future. By the end of this chapter, however, you will have a much deeper understanding of the money-generating side of your business.

Do you know how many customers you have in any given year? Or what they spend on average when they come to see you? Or even how often they come?

Understanding the breakdown of your current revenue stream is critical to preparing a growth plan. How will you know what needs changing if you don't know what it looks like today?

We will start by gathering as much information as possible from your historical financial information.

How Many Customers Do You Have?

If you have a business where you invoice customers in your accounting system, then you should be able to print off a listing of your current customers. If you use a manual invoicing system, however, it may take some work to come up with a customer count. Start by assembling all your invoices for the last 12 months. It doesn't matter if this time period is not the same as your fiscal year end. We are looking for the most current customer information. Sort your invoices by customer name as opposed to date. Then simply count how many different customers there are.

What do you do if you have a retail store where all your customers pay cash and you do not track their names? In this case, it pays to do a little research. For the next month, survey all customers that come into the store. Hand out a short survey form for them to fill out as your cashier is ringing up the purchases. A survey form might look like the one in Sample 8.

Keep in mind that the length of the survey can't be onerous to the customer or he or she won't participate. For example, customers in restaurants have more time to fill out a survey than convenience store customers do. Keep it short and as simple as possible.

Think about all the information this form gives you. If your customers have given you their names and addresses, you can begin a mailing list to let them know about specials and new products. Knowing if it's their first time visiting your store that month lets you know how many customers came into the store the entire month (you will simply count all the survey forms that have "yes" on this line). Knowing how many times they come in per month allows you to extrapolate how many times your customers see you every year. The final three questions give you some feedback about who your competitors actually are and how you stack up in comparison.

Once you have tracked the surveys for a month, you are ready to do your customer count. Simply count all the surveys where the customer has answered "yes" to the question "Is this your first time in the store this month?" and multiply that number by 12. For example, if 86 people said that it was their first time that month in the store, you would multiply 86 by 12 months to come up with an estimated average of 1,032 customers per year.

CASE STUDY

"Here's a really good example of what you're talking about," Becky said, pulling an invoice from the top of the pile. Vivian had been explaining to Becky and Joe that they needed to understand more about their current customer base before they could grow.

Joe scanned the invoice and groaned. "Not her again! What's the problem this time?"

"Remember when she called you to come out and find out what that smell was in the kitchen sink, you didn't find any problem. She doesn't think that she should be billed for the service call."

Joe banged his fist on the desk. "I made it clear to her before I went out there that she would pay a service call fee."

"I know," said Becky, shrugging her shoulders at Vivian. "She's always complaining about something."

Vivian said, "There are always going to be some people who will be unhappy no matter what. They're just difficult to deal with. Have you considered firing her?"

Joe laughed. "Firing her? That would be great if we could do it."

"Of course you can," said Vivian. "In the time that's being taken up dealing with her, how many regular, well-paying customers could you have serviced?"

"A whole bunch, that's for sure," Becky said. "It seems like we're always arguing with her on the telephone no matter what."

Vivian said, "Let's go through this same type of analysis on all of your customers. Let's find out who your good customers really are."

Sample 8
CUSTOMER SURVEY FORM

1. Name (optional): _____

2. Address (optional):_____

   _____

3. Is this your first time in the store this month? _____

4. How many times on average do you come here every month?_____

5. What other similar stores do you visit? _____

   _____

6. Is there anything that you feel we should be doing better?_____

   _____

   _____

7. What are the things that you enjoy about coming here? _____

   _____

   _____

How Often Do Your Customers Come to See You?

Now that we know how many customers we have, we need to find out how often they come to see us. If you have a computerized accounting system, such as *QuickBooks* or *Simply Accounting*, this information is easily attainable. From the Reports menu, find a report that details billings by customer. Your report might look something like Sample 9. (The report was generated in *QuickBooks* so yours might look a little different.)

What we want to do with this report is to count how many invoices we have issued. Another way of getting at this information is to subtract the invoice number on your first invoice in the 12-month period from the invoice number on the last invoice in the 12-month period. For example, if your first invoice number in the year is 953 and your last one is 1712, you have issued 759 invoices for the year. In other words, your customers have transacted with you 759 times. This second method will only work if you have issued sequential invoice numbers throughout the period and have not voided or deleted any invoices.

Once you know how many invoices you have issued in the past 12 months, simply divide that number by your customer count. Following the above example, if you have 547 customers and 759 invoices, then your customers come to see you approximately 1.4 times per year.

Sample 9
BILLINGS BY CUSTOMER REPORT

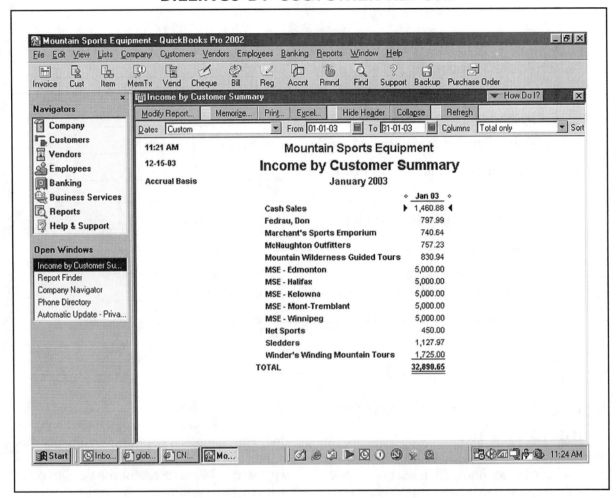

If you run a retail outlet, then we will go back to the survey result to come up with our estimate. You have already added up all the customers who have indicated that it is their first time that month in the store. Using only those surveys, add the cumulative number of times that these customers say they come into the store every month. Let's look at a simplified example:

Customer	1st time?	# times
John	yes	3
Mary	yes	2
Jake	yes	1
Fred	yes	6

Assuming that these are the only four customers to visit your store that month, the total number of visits is 3 + 2 + 1 + 6 = 12, and therefore, your customers visited you an average of 12 ÷ 4 = 3 times that month. To get to an annual average you would multiply by 12 months. In this example, your customers would visit you an average of 3 X 12 = 36 times per year. This would be typical for a convenience or grocery store.

What Do Your Customers Spend?

Now that we know how many customers we have and how often they come to see us, we need to find out what they're spending. This is a fairly easy process for most small businesses. Review your revenues for the past 12 months. Are there any billings in there that are unusual and might spike the results? For example, did you put a special order in for a customer for a large amount of product? If this is not likely to repeat, then we want to remove it from our calculations, otherwise our averages will be unnaturally high. This process is called normalizing the revenues, or, making them normal.

Once you have what you think is a good approximation of your current revenues, divide the revenue by your customer count. For example, if you have 650 customers and your revenues last year were $127,500, then your average revenue per customer is —

$127,500 ÷ 650 = $196.15 annual revenue per customer

One more calculation needs to be added, however, to get to the revenue per transaction as opposed to the revenue per customer. You now divide your revenue per customer by the average number of times your customers come to see you. Following the above example, if your customers come to see you an average of 3.2 times per year, your average transaction is:

$196.15 ÷ 3.2 = $61.30 per transaction

Therefore, in this example, you have 650 customers who come to see you an average of 3.2 times per year and they spend an average of $61.30 every time they come to see you.

What Kind of Customers Do You Have?

All small businesses go through it at some point or another. They have to face a customer that they just can't make happy regardless of how much they try. Some customers are just destined to complain, berate, not pay in a timely manner, and waste your time. Unfortunately, if you are like many small businesses, you will spend proportionately more time with this type of customer trying to pacify and satisfy him or her. The customer is always right, right?

Not necessarily. Take a few moments and jot down some notes about your ideal customer. What would make him or her ideal? Here are some things that my clients tell me are important to them:

- Paying on time without being reminded
- Being appreciative of the work you've done on their behalf
- Not complaining continually
- Recommending you to others
- Not being price-sensitive (understanding value)
- Making the work you do for them as easy as possible for you

Pull out your customer list again and review it. Place an "A" beside all of your customers that most closely resemble your ideal customer. Now place a "D" beside those customers that make you cringe when they walk through the door or call you on the phone. These customers are the opposite of your "A" customers. Of those customers that are left on your list, break them into two categories, "B" and "C", depending on whether they are closer to your "A" customers or your "D" customers respectively.

Obviously, you want to concentrate on your "A" and "B" customers. These are the customers that pay well, don't complain, and, best of all, refer other "A" and "B" customers to you. Spending your time with the "D" customers, however, hinders your ability to do this.

What would your business be like if your "D" customers went to one of your competitors? I know, that's not a very nice thing to do to another business! The thought of these customers leaving may scare you at first; nobody likes to lose a customer, but think about how much more free time you would have to be able to service your "A" and "B" customers. You'll also have more time to plan and strategize to make sure that your growth plan is working. Not to mention the fact that you will see morale in your business increase once the "problem" customers are out the door. I have seen this happen dozens of times over.

Fire Away!

So, what do you do about your "D" customers? Fire them! You heard me right: Fire them. You *do* have the ability to not agree to provide products or services to anyone you choose. Sample 10 is an example of a letter you can adapt to your own needs to send to those customers with whom you do not wish to do business any longer.

Once you have weeded out your more difficult customers, you will be well positioned to start growing your business with many more "A" and "B" customers. The improvement to the bottom line will be staggering!

The Next Step

In this chapter, we have learned how to get a handle on our historical customer information. Now is a good time to assess whether your accounting software is giving you the type of information that you need to run your business effectively. You will need to access this type of financial information on a regular basis. If you need to upgrade your record keeping software, you may wish to refer back to the first book in the *Numbers 101 for Small Business* series, *Bookkeepers' Boot Camp* for a fuller discussion of some considerations that you need to take into account as you are selecting a new system.

Now that we understand where our business has been in the past and we have weeded out the "bad apples," it's time to start our growth plan and test the impact that those changes have made.

Sample 10
TERMINATING A CUSTOMER

15 January 20--

Mr. John Doe
275 Clutterbuck Place
Joshua, MN 99506

Dear John,

There are times when every business needs to take some time and review their interactions with their customers, as well as look towards the future path.

That is what we have done here at McManus Computer Consultants. We have reviewed the products and services that we have traditionally provided to our customers and we have made some difficult decisions.

We have come to the realization that in order to provide the best and most comprehensive service to our customers, we must offer more services to fewer customers.

We have reviewed the history of the services that we have provided to you since you have been with us and we feel that your needs would be best served by another computer consulting firm. We would be happy to refer you to one if you wish.

We wish you all the best in the future!

Sincerely,

Michael McManus

McManus Computer Consultants

Checklist 6
GETTING A HANDLE ON YOUR REVENUES

1. I have set up a system to track information about my customers: their frequency, their purchases, and their habits. ☐

2. I know how many customers I have. ☐

3. I know how much my customers spend on average. ☐

4. I know how often my customers come to my business. ☐

5. I have rated my customers based on criteria such as the ease of serving them, the amount they spend, and their payment and referral history. ☐

6. I have considered firing my less desirable customers. ☐

7. I have reviewed my initial choice of accounting software and have ensured that it still meets my needs. ☐

Chapter Summary

➡ Your revenue stream is made up of a combination of how many customers you have, how often they come to see you, and how much they spend every time they come through the door.

➡ For most small businesses (except retail), your bookkeeping system should provide all the information you need to analyze your revenue streams.

➡ Consider weeding out your "D" quality customers to free up more of your time for planning and strategizing.

➡ Consider upgrading your bookkeeping system if information about revenues is not readily accessible.

Your Strategy

We have spent a great deal of time so far in this book laying the foundation for growth. This is time well spent because many small businesses make the mistake of growing unchecked without any idea as to where they've been or where they are going. We started by looking at the benefits of "systematizing" our business: Developing processes and procedures that can be followed and duplicated with consistency. We then reviewed our business and personal goals to make sure that our growth plan will dovetail with those goals. We've looked at the importance of profitable growth as well as the quality of our customers. Now we are finally ready to put our growth plan in place, from the top down.

Your Business's Vision Statement

Your business's vision statement formalizes those business goals that we discussed in

Chapter 21. The vision statement is an overall picture of what the business will look like in the future. It addresses who you are, what you're about, and how you will get there. Sample 11 gives two examples of effective vision statements.

First, the vision statement talks about the niche that the business will occupy. Are you the most knowledgeable? Or the most full-service? Do you have the widest selection? This is your niche and will be an integral part of your vision.

Second, the vision statement outlines in general terms how the business will accomplish its goals. What is it that will make you the best? How will you meet your customers' expectations? The vision statement is the skin in which your business will operate in the future. Its audience is the business owner, the employees, the customers, and the suppliers; in short, everyone who comes into contact with the business.

Sample 11
VISION STATEMENTS

Vision Statement 1

In ten years, we will be the most recognized computer consulting firm in our area of operation. Our revenues will grow to $1.2 million and we will maintain an aggressive growth rate of 20 percent per year, focusing only on profitable growth. The firm will be a fun place to work for both owners and employees. Employees will be compensated based on performance and alignment to the vision statement. The firm will hire only the best and brightest in the computer consulting field and these employees will receive outstanding training and work experience as well as long-term growth opportunities. All of this will be accomplished with absolute integrity and fairness to all those who interact with us.

Vision Statement 2

Kelly's Convenience Store will be Kensington Market's neighborhood grocery. We will stock a wide variety of products needed by customers on a regular basis and we will carry only the freshest fruits and vegetables. Our employees will be friendly and knowledgeable and will actively assist customers with their grocery purchases. Our loyal customer base will grow by 15 percent per year as new customers move into the area and as the neighborhood grows to value the store.

The Mission Statement

The purpose of the mission statement is to bring the general values of the vision statement down into measurable, concrete goals. In order for a mission statement to be effective, it needs to meet six criteria. Your mission statement must be —

- **Measurable.** You need to be able to determine if the goals are being met on a regular basis.

- **Challenging.** The goals should be a stretch to reach, but not unrealistic or unattainable.

- **Focused.** You will be using the mission statement to make operational and strategic decisions in your business so the goals need to be sharply focused.

- **Flexible.** The goals should allow for individual interpretation within the framework originally envisioned.

- **Clear.** One of the most important facets of the mission statement is its ability to be explained and understood by everyone in the organization. Therefore the goals should be easy to understand and not marred with "business speak."

- **Appropriate.** The goals in the mission statement must work towards achievement of the vision statement. If the mission statement is not in perfect alignment with the vision statement, the overall goals will not be achieved and the business will be dysfunctional.

Sample 12 shows a mission statement related to the vision of the computer consulting firm above.

Notice how the mission statement in Sample 12 takes each item in the vision statement and tells "how" the business is going to meet its vision goals. Once your mission statement has been developed, it needs to be drilled down even farther into individual operational tasks.

Your Operational Plan

In order for the mission statement goals to be implemented consistently, it's important to break them down even further into individual tasks with the names of the employees whose responsibility is to carry out each one, as well as specific timelines and measurements.

Let's have a look at the first mission statement goal in Sample 12. The associated operational tasks might look like this:

1. We will develop and maintain a highly visible community presence and will be known as a community-based business.

CASE STUDY

Becky made a face. "A vision statement? That sounds so formal! Do we really have to go through all that for such a small business?"

"The whole point is that you will be growing into a much larger business," said Vivian, "and it's important to lay the groundwork properly. We've already analyzed where you've been, now we have to look forward to where you're going."

Joe said, "Well, we already know that we want to have a million dollars in revenue in ten years and that we will be growing 18 percent per year to do that. That's a start."

"Yes," said Vivian, "now let's talk about your business's community profile and services. Let's look at what Joe's Plumbing stands for."

Sample 12
MISSION STATEMENT

1. In ten years, we will be the most recognized computer consulting firm in our area of operation.

   We will develop and maintain a highly visible community presence and will be known as a community-based business.

   Our marketing and promotional material will be distinctive and will be highly visible in all of our customers' places of business.

2. Our revenues will grow to $1.2 million and we will maintain an aggressive growth rate of 20 percent per year, focusing only on profitable growth.

   We will actively seek new customers through our interactions with our existing customers.

   We will strive to provide the best service to our select group of customers, turning them into not only loyal customers, but also advocates for us.

3. Our firm will be a fun place to work for both owners and employees.

   We will solicit employee feedback and input on all business matters.

   We will create a casual yet professional working environment where employees feel comfortable and productive.

4. Employees will be compensated based on performance and alignment with the vision statement.

   We will develop and maintain a world-class performance and evaluation system in which employees participate in both the risks and rewards of the business.

   We will clearly communicate our vision and mission statements with all employees on a regular basis.

5. The firm will hire only the best and brightest in the computer consulting field, and these employees will receive outstanding training and work experience as well as long-term growth opportunities.

   We will become the computer consulting firm of choice for new college graduates and those seeking employment in our industry.

Sample 12 — Continued

We will develop and maintain a world-class employee training system as well as thorough and clear documentation of every process and procedure in the business.

6. All of this will be accomplished with absolute integrity and fairness to all those who interact with the business.

We will review our operations on a monthly basis with all employees.

We will send feedback request forms to all customers at least annually to ensure that the customers' needs are being not only met, but also surpassed.

2. We will enter a corporate team in the Chamber of Commerce charity relay annually.

3. We will develop and maintain a charitable giving program whereby all donations made through the program by our customers or employees are matched by the business. This program will be put in place by April 30.

4. We will actively seek other opportunities to provide a visible community presence and will solicit input from our employees.

Notice how the mission statement goal has been broken down further to tell exactly how the business will accomplish the goal. These operational goals should become a part of the management operational plan that is followed on a consistent basis. See the second book in the *Numbers 101 for Small Business* series, *Financial Management 101*, for a fuller discussion of developing the management operational plan.

Vision Statement

Joe's Plumbing will provide its customers with top-notch service, as evidenced by its highly skilled plumbers helping customers in a polite and efficient manner. We will be the largest locally owned plumbing business in the tri-state area with annual revenues of over $1 million.

All Joe's Plumbing team members will work in an environment filled with mutual respect, trust, and absolute fun. All team members will be compensated well, based on individual and team performance, and will have access to continuous training and learning.

CASE STUDY

Becky finished reading the final draft of the vision statement out loud to Joe and Vivian.

"I feel like we're a bigger business already," Joe said. "But it's going to take a lot of work to become the business that's on that piece of paper."

Vivian said, "You're right, Joe. It will take a lot of work. But you have the framework in place already. Now we have to break the vision down into its component parts."

Checklist 7
YOUR STRATEGY

1. I have articulated the niche in which my business operates. ☐

2. I have analyzed my company's unique qualities in relation to my competitors. ☐

3. I have developed and recorded a formal vision statement for my business. ☐

4. I have broken the general values in my vision statement down into measurable, concrete goals in my mission statement. ☐

5. I have reviewed my monthly management operating plan to ensure that it fits in with the company's mission and vision statements. ☐

6. I have assigned responsibilities and deadlines to all tasks in my management operating plan. ☐

7. I have set up a review system to ensure that the tasks assigned in my management operating plan get completed. ☐

Chapter Summary

➡ Before your growth plan is put in place, it's important to make sure that the plan will help you meet your business and personal goals.

➡ Your vision statement is an umbrella statement that represents your business goals.

➡ Your mission statement takes the overall vision and breaks it into concrete, measurable pieces.

➡ The mission statement is further broken down into operational tasks, with deadlines and responsibilities attached.

Chapter

24

Testing Change

In the last chapter, we stressed the importance of having measurable goals so that you know if you are in alignment with the business's vision. In this chapter, we look at how to test and measure your growth plan and what to do if it needs adjustment.

Not understanding what impact every facet of their business has on profitability contributes to the downfall of thousands of businesses every year. Most small-business owners rely on their own faulty intuition or "gut feel" about what effect a new ad or a new product will have on their customers or revenues. Marketers often say, "I know I'm wasting half of my advertising dollars. I just don't know which half." This attitude results in overspending on marketing and promotion in an effort to hit the target with a "splatter gun" approach.

Measuring the results of changes in your business is the only way to know that you are still on the right path. It allows you to zero in on the least expensive and most productive growth strategies. You can measure everything, including prices, advertising, sales presentation methods, employee compensation

packages, and the mix of products and services that you offer. A business should integrate continual measuring and testing its entire life. That will ensure that the business continually grows and improves over time. Let's look at some of the different areas where measuring and testing are critical.

Advertising

Print and radio advertising can be the most expensive part of your marketing and promotion campaign. And if you're large enough to have a television advertising budget, well, the cost can be astronomical.

It doesn't seem to make sense, then, that most small businesses never know what, if any, benefits they are getting from their advertising campaigns. The cost of this ignorance can be enormous. It is estimated that one-half to two-thirds of all advertising dollars may just as well have been set on fire with a match!

Let's start with the basics: Do you know where your new customers are coming from? Telephone book ads? Word of mouth? Networking? For example, let's say you were spending $2,000 per year to have a display ad in the telephone book. Through analyzing your customer base and finding out where customers first heard about your business, you discover that only three percent of your customers found you in the telephone book. Most of your customers come in through referrals from existing customers or other associates. What impact will this have on your advertising budget? Are you likely to spend $2,000 next year to get only a few more customers? Not likely. You will have saved that $2,000 from going up in smoke and will still have almost the same number of customers. This illustrates why testing and measuring the results of your advertising campaigns can be very lucrative for your business.

Once you know where your customers are coming from, it's time to analyze the effectiveness of how you market to them. If most of your customers come in through referrals, one of your growth strategies may be to actively pursue your business contacts to solicit referrals. It's important to know how effective this change has been on your number of customers and your revenue. For example, let's say you send a mailing to your existing customers with a business card and an offer of 50 percent off their next visit to you if they bring in a new customer. It's a very simple matter of tracking how many new customers come in as referrals of existing customers. If your program only results in one new customer for every 100 letters you send to existing customers, then you know that the campaign has not been very effective. This will let you modify the campaign to improve its effectiveness. Try it again with 75 percent off the next visit or change the wording of the letter. But remember to only change one variable at a time so that you know when you've hit upon a winning idea.

This also works with print, radio, and television advertising. Every piece of advertising should be measurable. It is a well-known marketing truism that different headlines can have a dramatic impact on customer responses. Test the effectiveness of your headlines, make changes, and test again. See how many responses the ads pull and what the conversion ratio is. (The conversion ratio is the number of inquiries from the ad that turn into paying customers. We will cover this concept in more detail in Chapter 26.).

CASE STUDY

"How are we going to know if these changes we're making are working?" asked Becky.

Vivian sat down at the desk across from Becky. "Before you make any changes to your business, you need to set up a system to track the results of the changes. This way, you'll always know if the changes are having a positive, negative, or inconsequential impact on your revenues."

"How do we track something like that?" asked Becky. "Some of the changes we're making, like how we answer the telephone or our new advertising campaign, can't really be measured."

"Actually, they can," Vivian said. "There are many ways to measure the results of changes that you make to your operations. The key is to change only one variable at a time, so that you can isolate its effect. It's kind of like the experiments you did in high school science."

Becky frowned. "I was never very good in science," she said.

"Well, once we know what we want to track and we have the tracking system set up, it will happen almost automatically," said Vivian. "Then you can forget everything you learned about scientific experimentation."

If you are running different ad campaigns, have a unique identifier so that you know from which initiative the customer arrives. For example, you can include a coupon that must be returned. The coupons in each campaign would be unique, so that you can see that, for example, 20 new customers came from this ad and 57 came from that ad. You could also set up a different toll-free number for the potential customers to call depending on which ad they are responding to.

If you think that these measurement and testing techniques are too time-consuming or expensive, think about how much business and advertising money you are losing because you don't know what works.

Prices

When it comes to testing prices, many small-business owners put on the brakes. "Oh no, we have to charge this. If we change our prices, we'll lose all our business to our competitors." Again, this is a "gut feel" statement and may not bear any relation to facts.

The price that you charge for your product or service relates to the value equation: Value = Benefits ÷ Cost. (We will discuss this value equation in more detail in Chapter 25.)

The more perceived benefits to the customer versus the cost of the product or service, the higher the value the customer will place on it. Many small businesses tend to under-value their own products and services and charge too little for the value the customer receives.

There is another variable in the value perception, however. It is the perception that cheaper goods are low quality. Let me give you the real-life example of one of my clients.

Jim (not his real name) owns a small café in the trendy Queen Street West area of Toronto. He has 11 tables and a bar area. When Jim took over the business from the retiring

owner, at first he kept everything the same. The menu had changed little in almost 20 years. The café served diner-style food: large servings, simple ingredients, low prices. The area that Jim had turned into a bar had been a lunch counter. The restaurant was frequently operating at capacity. The tables were always full at both lunch and dinner. By most accounts, the restaurant was a huge success. The problem that jumped out at Jim after a short while was that his profits were dismal. He was paying an exorbitant rent typical for that neighborhood. He just wasn't able to turn over the tables fast enough to meet his costs. Something had to change quickly.

Jim was acutely aware of the value equation. He knew that the area in Toronto that he was operating in was famous as a "destination." People browse Queen West for its trendy bars, art galleries, and clubs. The popularity of the area and its reputation was one of the reasons that Jim's rent was so high.

Ultimately, Jim knew that he had to change his prices to be able to survive. He knew that this meant that people's perceptions of the café had to change. The first thing he did was to paint and renovate the interior to reflect a comfortable but upscale environment. He applied for and received a liquor license and converted the lunch counter into a bar and lounge area. The next thing he did was to consult with his kitchen staff about the menu. Jim knew that he wanted to offer customers a better dining experience and thereby be able to command higher prices.

In the end, Jim altered the menu to include many dishes that still had simple ingredients but were prepared in a more "upscale" fashion and had "trendier" names. He was able to increase his prices by an average of 112 percent with only an additional 16 percent in cost. And the cafe was still full every lunch and dinner. Had Jim not been successful in his first testing of his price changes, he would have adjusted the menu and pricing again until it had the desired effect on revenues. Jim has since purchased four other restaurants in Toronto and has revamped them in a similar manner. In three of these cases, he had to alter his original plan based on testing his prices. With all five of his restaurants, he will continually test his strategies and make the changes he needs to always be improving quality and the bottom line.

It's important to remember that, for example, a 10 percent increase in prices does not always equate to an equal and offsetting decrease in customers. You need to test the changes that you can make in prices without losing business.

Environment

The environment in which you and your employees work can have a huge impact on your revenues, both from an internal and an external perspective. Internally, how your employees feel about coming to work every day can affect their morale and motivation — which can affect how they do their jobs and interrelate with customers. Externally, customers make unconscious conclusions about a business by the environment in which it operates.

The example that I will give you about internal environment issues relates to my own experience. While I was articling with accounting firms to receive my accounting designation, I worked in some very different environments. Some of the firms were extremely informal: They were loud and raucous, had no dress code, and had a refrigerator full of beer. There was no hierarchy and employees had complete freedom to manage our own time. Some of the firms were diametrically opposite: They were silent, formal environments where employees did not speak to the partners unless it was vital. We wore formal business attire and spoke with fellow workers with short monotone sentences, always related to work, never to hockey or reality TV shows or our families.

Both of the extremes in which I worked affected the firms. In a completely anarchistic workplace, it is sometimes difficult to switch from being laid back and informal to listening to client needs and being respectful. On the other hand, in a rigid, severe atmosphere, a client may perceive us as being rigid in our thinking and advice. When I started my own accounting firm, I tried to strike a balance between these models: informal enough to encourage original thought, but structured enough to focus on client needs. I tested and adjusted the rules for our working environment until the business was successful, as evidenced by employee retention and client happiness.

The external environment can have an even more direct impact on the operations and, ultimately, revenues of a business. Customers make subconscious conclusions about the quality and professionalism of a business by the first impressions formed when first entering the business's environment.

The next time you walk into a new business, whether it be a retail store, a supplier or your local dry cleaners, consciously think about the first impressions that form as you enter. Is the entry area clean and tidy? What do you smell? Is the area set up for the benefit of the customer or the staff? Is the waiting area soothing, with soft colors and calming music, or chaotic, with ringing telephones and employees yelling? Businesses that make the effort to set up their operations for the benefit and comfort of their customers develop loyal customers.

How can you do this in your own business? First, think about how you like to be welcomed into the companies with which you interact. What does the environment look like?

What sounds and smells greet you? Incorporate these elements into your own business and test the response. There are many ways to do this, but these are the two main ones:

- Track comments made by customers when they enter the environment for the first time. If it's a positive environment, you may hear comments such as "Take your time. I'm enjoying the wait." or "I always feel so comfortable here." Although these are subjective measures of success, they are still important to track.

- Solicit more formal feedback. At the end of every customer interaction, provide a short survey for customers to fill out, indicating anything they particularly enjoyed or wanted to have changed concerning many aspects of your business, including the operating environment.

If you find that customers do not talk about the comfort of your environment, through either informal conversation or formal survey, make changes to the environment and test again. Continue to improve and retest until your test results cannot be improved by any other changes you make. This way, you'll always be improving your customers' impressions of your business and will be making changes when necessary.

Checklist 8
TESTING CHANGE

1. I know from where my new customers are being referred. ☐

2. I know how many new customers each of my advertising and marketing campaigns are yielding. ☐

3. I have developed a system to measure the response to every new advertising initiative. ☐

4. I have reviewed all of the prices of my goods and services to ensure that they will meet market expectations. ☐

5. I have thought about the type of atmosphere in which I want my staff to operate and which I want clients to experience. ☐

6. I have documented the specific tasks related to my marketing and promotional strategy. ☐

7. I have documented the specific tasks related to making the operating environment of my business comfortable and hospitable to staff and customers. ☐

Chapter Summary

➡ You can't know if your business is on the right track unless you test and measure every change you make to your operations.

➡ You can measure the effectiveness of your advertising by having unique response coupons or codes so that you can tell from which piece of advertising a response comes.

➡ The impact of changes to prices can be measured directly by their impact on revenues.

➡ The way your customers perceive your environment can also be measured by informally tracking customer comments or formally tracking survey responses.

Chapter

25

Your Product or Service

In this chapter, we are going to look at your offerings as a business, regardless of whether you offer a product or service. *What* you offer and *how* you present it can make a substantial difference in your revenues. Remember from Chapter 21 that the three ways to grow a business are —

- Attract new customers
- Sell them more every time they come
- Get them to come more often

Also, remember that, in order to get leveraged growth, we need to concentrate simultaneously on all three areas.

Why Should Customers Buy from You?

This is a question that you have asked yourself as part of developing your vision and mission statements (see Chapter 23). What makes you different from your competitors and sets you apart? When potential customers consider making a new purchase, why would they consider your business? There are really only two bases upon which you can compete in business: Price and value.

Competing on price

"THE LOWEST PRICE IN TOWN"

"WE MATCH ALL COMPETITORS' PRICES"

"NOBODY BEATS US . . . NOBODY!"

I'm sure you've seen headlines like this in the advertising section of your local newspaper. In fact, take a few minutes right now and look through the sales flyers in the newspaper. How many businesses are advertising that their price is the best?

Many small businesses feel that they have to compete on price alone; that customers will only come and buy from you if you are the cheapest. What this ends up doing is starting a downward cycle, where each business in an industry undercuts the other until there are no margins left, and businesses start going bankrupt or leaving the industry.

If you think that you can undercut all your competitors, think again. There will always be new competitors in the market who can undercut you. New competitors have the benefit of still having their start-up financing in place and can price almost at cost for however long they feel it will take to yank your customer base out from under you.

Something else to consider is that the type of customer that buys from you solely on price will jump to a competitor in a heartbeat if the competitor's prices are lower. There is no customer loyalty at this end of the market. It can make for some very hard slogging on your part just to keep your proverbial head above water if you are going to compete on price.

Competing on value

The other niche upon which you can base your business is adding value. We discussed this concept briefly in Chapter 24. By far, the largest segment of consumers doesn't simply want the cheapest price regardless. They want to know that they are getting value for their money. It's not that they want to pay more if they don't have to, but they understand that cheaper isn't always better. Customers define value as:

Benefits/Price

The higher the perceived benefits to the customer versus the price of a product or service, the more likely he or she is to purchase. Notice that we are speaking of "perceived benefits." That means that the customer needs to believe he or she is getting the best product or service for the best price. Getting that value perception across to customers is one of the most important jobs of a business.

My experience has shown me that most small businesses are terrified to compete on value, because it is so ingrained in them that they have to cut prices to stay in business. But think about how wonderful it would be to get a higher price for your product or service, provide better quality to your customers, and have them appreciate what you provide to them. That's the outcome of competing on value.

How Is Your Business Different?

Consumer theory shows that customers buy value that they perceive. What this means is

---

CASE STUDY

"Ok. So, now can we start actually working on our growth plan?" Joe asked.

"Joe, don't be so impatient," Becky said. "It takes time to do things the right way. Remember, we want to grow this company into a million-dollar asset." She turned to Vivian. "But I'm really looking forward to actually putting this plan in place."

Vivian sipped her coffee. "We're just about there. We know how much we're going to grow and the basics of how to grow. Now we need to have a look at the services that you provide to your customers and see where you can increase sales."

Joe frowned. "How can we do that? The way it works is that, if customer need plumbing work done, they call us. We can't predict when someone's drain is going to back up."

Vivian said, "Let's start by making a list of all the services that you have provided over the last year. I think you'll find some interesting patterns emerging."

that if they feel that the benefits of your product or service outweigh its cost by a higher margin than your competitors (assuming, of course, that it's a product or service that they need), then they will buy that perceived value. Remember from the above section that value to a customer is defined as:

Benefits/Price

Articulating your product or service's value, however, runs much deeper than your advertising campaign. It needs to be at the heart of your business. It is embedded in your vision and mission statements, and it needs to be communicated indirectly to customers through every interaction that you have with them.

Does the value you bring to the table have to be completely different than any other business in your industry? Of course not. You simply have to articulate it better.

For example, FedEx's slogan (and, in fact, the core of their entire business) is —

Absolutely Positively Overnight

Are they the only courier company on the planet that can deliver packages overnight? Of course not! But they articulate it better than anyone else. It's clear to their customers and potential customers that they will get it there by tomorrow morning. And, of course, that's extremely important to customers of the courier industry.

So, how can you articulate the value that your business provides? What makes you stand out from your competitors? Do you have the most experience in the industry? Are you the most full- service?

Once you have determined your value statement, make sure that it permeates all your correspondence and internal processes and procedures. Make it the very core of your operations.

Let's look at some hands-on ways that you can increase your revenues by focusing on your customers' perceived value of your product or service.

Selling a Product

In general, it is easier to communicate to potential customers the value of a product than of a service. Customers can see and touch your product and will be able to compare it to the products your competitor offers.

However, it's critical to continually remind your customers and potential customers of the benefits of owning your product. For example, if you sell vacuum cleaners, remind them that, if they buy your vacuum cleaner, they —

- will never have to change a bag,
- will be able to vacuum their curtains with the special attachment, thereby saving money on dry cleaning, and
- will be able to tuck it away in a very small space when done, thereby saving them space.

It's an old marketing truism that customers buy benefits, not features, and it's a valuable one. What it means is that instead of listing all the bells and whistles of your product, tell your customers why they should care. Lead them by the hand to show them how much better their lives would be if only they owned your product. The benefits can even be ones that the customer would get if they bought your competitors' products. But if you're the company that can articulate those benefits the best, you will get the business.

Up Selling

You most likely have come across this term before. It means offering the customer more. McDonald's uses this strategy hundreds of thousands of times every day, whenever an employee says, "Would you like fries with that?"

To see another example, look at the area surrounding the checkout counter at any grocery store. The area will be filled with common useful items that almost everyone needs: batteries, light bulbs, camera film, and candy bars (okay, this one technically isn't a need, but it's something that people grab on impulse, especially if they are stuck in a checkout line). The grocery store is giving its customers one last opportunity to buy from them.

Take some time to examine the products that you offer and then list the related products and supplies that you could be offering. If you sell cameras, your customers will also need film, photo processing, frames, lenses, and camera bags. If these customers have to go elsewhere for these supplies, you are letting money walk out the door. They are already in front of you — do not be afraid to sell more to them.

You can also package these products together. In our camera example, instead of slashing the price of the camera to bring people in the door (competing on price), offer them a special deal: If they buy a camera from you, they will get a free camera bag and two rolls of film. This is showing the customer the value that they will receive. You will end up with much more revenue than you would if you simply cut your prices.

Providing a Service

Articulating the value of a service can be more difficult than doing so for a product. A product is tangible; it is something a customer can touch, see, and smell. They can assess the value fairly quickly and easily. A service, on the other hand, is intangible. When it has been completed, it may be difficult for the customer to know what value has been added. Therefore, it's critical to make sure that you define and communicate the value of your services.

Let's look at an example of two companies in the same industry: Landscaping. You are in need of some landscaping services around your house. You definitely need the grass cut on a regular basis and you might want some help with weeding flower beds and some ongoing lawn fertilizing and maintenance.

You call Lawn King, the first landscaping company listed in the Yellow Pages. This is the information they tell you over the telephone about their services:

- Lawn cutting costs $40 per hour. There is a minimum one-hour charge per cut and a minimum charge of $400 per year.
- Weeding and landscaping services cost $75 per hour. There is a minimum two-hour charge per visit.
- Other lawn maintenance services are by quotation and dependent upon the size of yard.

You then call Landscapes Galore to see how their services and prices stack up. They give you this information:

Lawn care package:
- Weekly lawn cutting from April to October
- Spring revitalization treatment including aerating, organic fertilizer, and weed removal
- Fall maintenance treatment including de-thatching and rooting fertilizer
- Cost: $375 due April 1 or four monthly payments of $100 beginning April 1
- Other services: Flower bed design consultation — $125
- Winter snow removal November to March — $225

Now, which company are you more likely to hire? The second one of course, and you may even decide to have them do your snow removal in the winter. Landscapes Galore has "productized" their service, which means that they have tried to make it as tangible as possible. They give you a fixed price and clearly state what you get for that price. Not only that, but they also clearly tell you what other bundles of services they provide to make it easier for you to decide whether or not you need those services.

The first company, Lawn King, is typical of many small businesses. They are so afraid of losing money on a sale that they hedge their bets. They quote by the hour and put in minimums. They also won't quote on other jobs without coming out to see them. The problem with this approach is that it makes the potential customer wary. The customer is not sure of the final bill and is therefore more reluctant to hire the company. What if it takes them six hours to cut the lawn!

How can you make your service more like a product? Consider the following strategy:

1. List all the services you provide or could provide. Only include those services that you and your staff are skilled at and enjoy doing.

2. Put together some "packages" of services that you feel would be of interest to your customers. Take some time to think about what your customers' needs are.

3. Work out what you feel would be the average charge to perform all these services. Look at how much time you think it would take to provide the services and price accordingly.

4. Communicate the packages to your existing customers. Let them know what else they can buy from you. They already like what you have to offer and they trust your quality and business ethics.

You can put a stronger push on these packages during your slow operating periods. For example, if your revenues are seasonal and usually decrease in the summer, offer the packages of services during that time to smooth out and boost your revenue streams.

Teaching Your Customers

Whether you sell a product or a service, one way you might consider adding to your revenues is by running workshops for your customers. People like to learn how to do things for themselves rather than being reliant upon others. This strategy can work in almost every industry. If you sell vacuums, you can run a half-day workshop on extending the life of your carpet. If you run a computer consulting business, you can teach customers more advanced computing skills, how to set up their own database, or a myriad of other computer skills. Customers will value learning these skills and you can price your workshops accordingly. It's a great way to boost your revenue throughout the year.

Checklist 9
YOUR PRODUCT OR SERVICE

1. I am able to articulate why my customers should
    buy from me rather than the competition. ❑

2. I have ensured that my growth strategy is based
    on competing on value, not on price. ❑

3. I have reviewed all of my marketing and promotional
    material to make sure that they embody the value
    that my product or services bring to my customers. ❑

4. I have analyzed which of my products or services
    are a natural fit with each other. ❑

5. I have documented my plan for presenting products
    and services to my customers that are a natural fit with
    the ones they are purchasing. ❑

6. I have "productized" the services I offer so that
    customers can easily see their value. ❑

7. I have considered providing training courses to my
    customers as an added source of revenue. ❑

Chapter Summary

➡ Competing on value rather than on price is the key to revenue growth.

➡ Focus on new products and services that you can offer your existing customers.

➡ If you sell a service, "productize" it; make it clear to your customers what they're getting and what they're paying.

➡ Consider increasing revenues by running workshops to teach your customers new skills related to your products or services.

Chapter

26

Your Customer Interactions

You can have the best product or service on earth and still not be able to attract or retain customers if you and your employees fail to develop good customer service skills. I'm talking about more than just being nice to people. I'm talking about the way customers view every single interaction with your business. How you interact with your customers can make a huge impact on your number of customers and the amount of revenue that they generate.

Telephone Interactions

Most small businesses are dependent upon the telephone to conduct their business and interact with customers and potential customers. Sample 13 shows two examples of how a small business might answer the telephone when a potential customer phones to inquire about the services the company offers.

Although these two telephone conversations are fictional, they are representative of the differences between businesses that do and do not understand the importance of every customer interaction.

Which business are you more likely to deal with? The second one, most likely. The employee was personable, knowledgeable, and helpful. He also knew the importance of closing the deal.

The Art of Closing the Deal

When we look at the first of the three ways to grow your business (see Chapter 21), attracting new customers, we can break that down further into two categories:

- Getting more potential customers in front of you

- Converting more potential customers into buyers

Let's say that you run a restaurant. More than 95 percent of your business comes from people calling in to make reservations. People

Sample 13
TELEPHONE INTERACTIONS

Situation 1

Employee: **Taylor Hardware.**

Caller: Yes, hi. Could you tell me if you have any 12-foot 4X4 cedar in stock?

Employee: **Uh, yeah. We usually have some around.**

Caller: And how much is it?

Employee: **(shuffling paper) Uh, I think it's $37.50.**

Caller: Thanks.

Employee hangs up.

Situation 2

Employee: **Good morning, Greenplay Hardware, this is James.**

Caller: Hi, James, could you tell me if you have any 12-foot 4X4 cedar in stock?

Employee: **Sure, thanks for calling. It will just take me a moment to look it up on the screen. While I'm doing that, can I ask what type of project you need it for?**

Caller: I'm building a swing set for my kids. I have all the other wood, just not the crossbar.

Employee: **That sounds like an ambitious project! Just to let you know, we've just gotten in some new rope ladders that would be a great addition to any swing set. When you drop in, just ask for me and I'd be happy to show them to you. Ah, here it is: 12-foot 4X4 cedar. We have over a dozen in stock. They're $37.50 each. Would you like me to set one aside for you?**

Caller: Sure, that would be great. The last name is Jones. I'll be in this afternoon and I would definitely like to see those rope ladders.

Employee: **Great. When you come in I will show you how to attach the ladder. It's really quite simple.**

Caller: Thanks, James. I'll see you this afternoon.

Employee: **Have a great day, Mr. Jones.**

who have never been in your restaurant before, however, want to ask some questions over the telephone before they decide that they want to make a reservation. They generally inquire about prices, seating, noise level, and menu.

Currently, out of every ten potential new customers who call, six make a reservation. This is your conversion ratio. The conversion ratio is calculated as:

Conversion ratio = People who buy ÷ People who inquire

Your conversion rate is therefore six divided by ten, or 60 percent. Your goal is to get more new customers who will come back again and again. There are two ways that you can get more new customers to make reservations:

1. You can get more people to call the restaurant.
2. You can convert more of the telephone inquiries into reservations.

Let's look at each of these in turn.

Getting more people to call

You can get more people to call your business through advertising or giving out coupons. One restaurant client of mine turns her existing customers into sales people for the restaurant. Current customers receive a free meal if they convince a friend or associate who has never been in the restaurant before to make a reservation. At first, you might think: Well, that doesn't do me any good. I'm losing the revenue on one meal to get the revenue on another.

CASE STUDY

"Hello. Joe's Plumbing," Becky said in answer to the ring of the telephone.

"Yes. My husband and I are building an addition on to our house. We're doing the general contracting ourselves and we need a plumber to come in to put in the fixtures in the new bathroom. Do you do that type of work?"

"Absolutely." Becky began to take notes.

"How much do you charge?"

"We charge $40 per hour. If you need a better idea of the cost, I can send Joe out to look at it for you."

"Um … does that visit cost anything?"

Becky answered, "No. Not at all."

"Well, let me discuss it with my husband and I'll get back to you."

"Okay. Thanks. Bye."

Becky hung up the phone. It would be nice to get in some more construction work before winter came. There was a knock on the office door.

"Vivian!" Becky said, opening the door. "It's great to see you. I had almost forgotten that we were going to work on the next phase of the growth plan this morning." She ushered Vivian into the room. "I just got a call from a potential new customer who needs some rough-ins done."

Vivian pulled her notebook from her briefcase. "You most likely wouldn't have gotten that job."

Becky looked puzzled. "What do you mean? How do you know that?"

Vivian said, "That was me. I wanted to experience first-hand how you handle a potential new customer. We have a lot of work to do."

But, if you look at the long-term potential of a new customer, you will realize that you are gaining a whole lot more. We will talk about the lifetime customer in Chapter 27.

Going back to our example, let's say in an average month, you have 75 potential new customers call the restaurant to make inquiries. At your current conversion rate of 60 percent, you would have 45 new customers.

75 inquiries X 60% conversion rate = 45 new customers

So, if we can increase the number of inquiries to 90, then we will have more customers.

90 inquiries X 60% conversion rate = 54 new customers

Definitely an improvement. However, if you do not simultaneously focus on increasing your conversion rate, you are also increasing the number of people who will *not* become customers. When you had 75 inquiries and were able to convert 45 of them into customers, you also had 30 people who telephoned your restaurant and decided to not become customers. When you start increasing the number of inquiries, you also increase the number of non-customers. We now have 36 people who will not become customers (90–54=36).

The danger of this is that people who are unsatisfied with a business tend to tell their friends and associates that they are unhappy. They might say things like, "I called the restaurant and they were really rude when I asked about vegetarian choices" or "When I called, they told me I couldn't get a reservation for another three weeks, so I called another restaurant."

The last thing that you want to be doing is increasing the number of people in your community who will never do business with you. That's why you must also focus on the second

method of attracting new customers.

Increasing your conversion rate

When a potential customer calls you on the telephone, he or she will decide in the space of a few moments whether or not to buy from you. What can you do to influence his or her decision? As we've seen from the two scenarios at the beginning of the chapter, the way the telephone is answered and the information provided has a huge impact on the buy/not buy decision. Try adopting the following characteristics during any telephone (or face-to-face) interaction with potential customers:

- **Be personable.** It doesn't matter if you're having a bad day and have too much work to do. There is nothing more important for your business than speaking with a customer or potential customer, so make sure that you are not coming across as rude on the telephone. Part of being personable means that the person on the other end of the telephone feels a connection to you. Always use your name so that the customer perceives that he or she is talking to a real person who cares about his or her questions and concerns.

- **Be attentive.** True listening is a skill that every business owner and customer service provider (i.e., your employees) must learn if your business is to be successful. Take the time to truly listen to your customers, whether they are asking questions, giving praise, or voicing a complaint. Repeat back to them their concerns so it is clear that you are genuinely trying to understand what they are telling you and also to make sure that you understand them correctly.

- **Be informative.** Make sure that even the most mundane telephone conversation with your potential customers gives them more information than they were expecting. This goes back to the concept of value that we discussed in earlier chapters. Customers need to feel that they are receiving value from the businesses that they interact with. If you are providing them with useful information when they are speaking with you for the first time, it will make an impression.

- **Close the deal!** Make it clear to potential customers that you want their business. ASK for their business! Use phrases like:

  - "So, for which evening would you like a reservation?"

  - "What day would work best for you to have the no-charge consultation?"

  - "Would you like to take the rope ladder with you as well?"

Don't be shy about letting your customers know that you want the business. It makes them feel appreciated and it can be the single best strategy for increasing your revenues.

So, how does your business stack up in the area of converting potential customers into customers? As always, it's important to analyze actual numbers rather than leaving it up to "gut feel."

For the next month, track all of your interactions with potential customers, whether by telephone, trade show, or through your business's front door. This also applies to the interactions each of your employees has with potential customers. You may want to adapt the form in Sample 14 to use.

Once you have tracked the interactions with your potential customers for the period of one month, you will have some good information that can help you make changes to your business. You will know how many opportunities you had to present yourself to new customers. You will also know what your potential customers ask you about. This will help you to prepare information for your employees to use in future interactions.

You will also be able to calculate an estimate of your conversion rate. Although it won't be perfect because it does not consider those customers who are only delaying their purchase instead of refusing to purchase, it will give you a good indication of how good your closing skills are.

To calculate your current customer conversion rate, simply take the number of forms on which the inquiry became a customer and divide it by the number of completed forms. For example, if you had a total of 57 filled-out forms and, of those, 22 people went on to become customers, then your conversion rate is:

$$22 \div 57 = 39\%$$

Using Scripts

Now that we've had a look at how to handle potential customer interactions and different ways of increasing the conversion rate, you need to decide what changes you want to make in your own business. If you go back and have another look at the franchise model in Chapter 19, you'll notice that all customer interactions are scripted; that is, they have been written out and memorized. At first, you may think that this might make your business impersonal and stilted, but, in fact, it will ensure that your message comes across consistently every time someone from your business interacts with a customer or potential customer.

Develop your own telephone script by writing down your ideal telephone call: One that is interactive, friendly, and results in a sale. Refer back to the section above on the art of closing the deal to understand what to include in the script.

Sample 14
POTENTIAL CUSTOMER INTERACTION REVIEW FORM

DATE: _____

TYPE OF INQUIRY *(circle one)*:
Telephone/In-person at office/In-person other/Email

CUSTOMER NAME: _____

INQUIRY SPECIFICS *(check as many as apply)*:

_____ Product or service specifics

_____ Pricing

_____ Hours of operation

_____ Experience

_____ How-to information

_____ Other (please elaborate) _____

Did customer agree to buy during the interaction? *(circle one)*: YES/NO

If no, why not? _____

_____

_____

Other relevant information_____

_____

_____

Becky said, "I guess I never really thought about how I answer the telephone. But I see now what a huge difference it makes to the customer."

"And to your bottom line," answered Vivian.

The office phone rang. Becky looked over at Vivian.

Vivian put her hands in the air. "It's not me this time. But can you put it on the speakerphone so I can hear?"

"Good morning. Joe's Plumbing. This is Becky."

"Hi, Becky. It's Mrs. Granger calling. I'm a little worried about the garbage disposal unit in my kitchen. It's making some strange noises. Do you think Joe could come out to have a look at it?"

"Thanks for calling, Mrs. Granger. Joe can certainly come out and have a look at it for you. There's a service that we provide that you might be very interested in. It's becoming very popular with customers such as yourself. It's called the Fall Maintenance Package. Joe will come out and inspect all of your visible plumbing, including the garbage disposal, to make sure that there are no blockages or leaks. He will look at the seals on the toilets to check that they're not breaking down and he will also drain your water heater. That will help to extend its life. The service costs $95 plus tax and it will give you some peace of mind knowing that everything has been looked at. Of course, if something is truly wrong with the garbage disposal, Joe will fix that while he's there. That repair will cost $40 per hour. Most garbage disposal repairs take less than two hours. Would you like to schedule a Fall Maintenance Package?"

"Oh, that sounds wonderful. Can Joe come out tomorrow sometime?"

Becky finished scheduling the appointment and smiled at Vivian as she hung up the telephone. "How did I do?" she asked.

"Much better. You closed the deal and sold a service that the customer didn't even know about when she first called. She's clearly happy with the appointment. It's a win-win situation. And Joe most likely would have done much of that work anyway as part of the service call. This way, he's getting paid for it."

Once you have developed your telephone script, meet with all of your employees who have access to interactions with your customers and train them on the script. Make sure that they understand enough about your product or service to be able to help your customers, whether it be by telephone or in person.

Sample 15 is the telephone script that I had all of my team members use in my accounting practice. You can alter it to suit your own needs.

You can see how this would make clients or potential clients react. They would know with whom they are talking because the staff member would have identified himself or herself. Even if the person they were looking for

wasn't available, the staff member who has picked up the telephone has asked if he or she could help the caller instead. This makes the clients feel as if the business cares above all else about their concerns and questions.

A Word about Screening Callers

"May I tell her who's calling?" This is a familiar phrase heard by customers on the telephone every day.

Many small businesses ask callers their names before they put them through to the staff member for whom they're asking. From a business's point of view, it allows the staff

Sample 15
TELEPHONE SCRIPT

Always answer telephone on the second ring.

Smile before you pick up the telephone (clients will hear it in your voice).

Good morning *(or afternoon)*, Mohr & Company, this is *(staff member first name, last name)*.

1. If person that the caller is looking for is available:

   Hi, *(client first name)*. Yes, she is available, I'll put you right through.

2. If person that the caller is looking for is not currently available:

   She's with someone at the moment. Is there some way that I can help?

(Assist caller as best you can. If you are unable to do so, let the caller know that you will leave a message with the staff member that the caller was originally looking for and that he or she will return the call within four business hours.)

Thanks for calling and have a great day!

---

member to be prepared for the caller and perhaps to assemble any files or other information that he or she needs to complete the call.

From a customer's perspective, however, this tactic is viewed as a method of figuring out if the caller is worth speaking to or not. It tends to create barriers between the customer and the business, something I recommend against when trying to build a business based on trust.

Actively screening a caller is unnecessary as well. Using the telephone script above, the staff member introduces himself or herself, thereby soliciting an introduction from the caller. Even if the caller doesn't identify himself or herself, technology now allows us to know the identity of callers through call display. So, we have thus eliminated the business reason for screening calls.

Tracking Conversion Rate Changes

We now know how to calculate your business's conversion rate and we've looked at some methods of improving that rate. As with any other change in your business, it is important to track the changes in your conversion rate that are due to changes in the way that you do business. For example, once your telephone scripts are in place, track your conversions using the same form that you used to calculate your original conversion rate. If you notice that there are no discernible changes in the rate, try some new changes to the telephone script and test the impact of those. Continually work on improving your customer closing skills and you will notice the impact on your revenues quickly.

Checklist 10
YOUR CUSTOMER INTERACTIONS

1. I have spent time examining other companies' telephone procedures. ❏

2. I have drafted a telephone script for my business and have documented procedures on how to handle telephone interactions with cutomers. ❏

3. I know what my current customer conversion ratio is. ❏

4. I have developed a plan to increase my business's conversion ratio. ❏

5. I have provided training to my employees on customer interactions. ❏

6. I actively work on my own listening skills to improve my customer interactions. ❏

7. I have developed methods to ask for a customer's business. ❏

Chapter Summary

➡ Seemingly small changes in the way that you and your staff interact with your customers can have a huge impact on customer acquisition and retention and, therefore, revenues.

➡ The first of the three ways to grow your business, attracting new customers, can be further broken down into the activities of getting more potential customers in front of you and increasing your conversion rate from potential customer to customer.

➡ To project a consistent message to your customers, develop a telephone script to be used by every staff member who has interaction with your customers and potential customers.

➡ It's important to understand your current conversion rate and to track the changes in your conversion rate due to changes in your business model.

Chapter
27

Your Marketing and Promotions

How much should you spend on trying to bring new customers in the door? In Chapter 21, we've seen that this approach is only one of three that we should be pursuing to grow your business. Yet, it's still an important one.

Many business "experts" will tell you that advertising costs should be a set percentage of your total expenses, somewhere between 3 percent and 5 percent. However, when you look at this approach more closely, you will realize that it does not make any intuitive sense. Advertising costs bear no relation to the other costs on your income statement. They are more closely related to your revenues, although this isn't always the case, either. Think about your business when you first started up. You had zero revenues and most likely a substantial advertising budget. That budget would not have changed in perfect step with the increases in revenue over time.

A more useful approach in deciding how much to spend on your advertising is to look at the lifetime value of your customers.

The Lifetime Value of a Customer

Understanding the true value of a customer assists you in managing your business. It allows you to more accurately predict your cash flows. It also lets you know how much to spend on advertising to bring in a similar customer.

Unfortunately, very few business owners think in terms of the lifetime value of their customers. They think only about the customer's initial purchase. Some businesses make the fatal mistake of treating their customers according to how much they spend when they first come through the door: Big customers get the "red carpet" treatment, and small ones get indifference. These businesses are missing a clear understanding of what that customer will bring in to the business over the long term.

The lifetime value of a customer is simply the amount of profit that the customer will add to your business over the length of the customer-supplier relationship.

Let's look at an example:

Janine owns a bottled-water company. She sells water coolers as well as five-gallon bottles of water. Her customers consist mostly of other small- and medium-size businesses that have standing orders for a set number of water bottles per week, which Janine's drivers deliver to the customers' place of business. The water coolers sell for $95, and each bottle of water sells for $5.25. Janine has calculated that her average customer purchases 2.5 bottles per week or 130 per year. The cost to Janine to purchase the water coolers is $63.50, the average cost of each bottle of water is $2.10, and the cost to deliver each bottle of water is $1.05.

When new customers come to see Janine, they usually purchase a cooler and a few bottles of water. Therefore, on the initial sale, Janine makes:

Water cooler:	($95.00 - $63.50)	**$31.50**
4 bottles of water: 4 @	($5.25 - $2.10 - $1.05)	**+ 8.40**
Total gross profit on sale:		**$39.90**

Basically, this is a $40 sale. If you were Janine, what would you spend to attract a $40 customer? Clearly less than $40. But Janine understands that this new customer is worth significantly more than that.

We know that, on average, a customer purchases 130 bottles per year. Janine has calculated that customers usually stay with her company at least three years. Therefore, the value of this customer to Janine is:

Initial sale:	**$39.90**
Ongoing water sales: ($2.10 gross profit per bottle X 130 bottles per year X 3 years)	**819.00**
Total gross profit:	**$ 858.90**

CASE STUDY

Becky pulled a brochure from her in-box and showed it to Vivian.

"The newspaper advertising rep came to see me yesterday. He wants to sell us a package of 12 weekly ads for $1,500. I think that it will be a great way to let people know about our new maintenance packages."

Vivian scanned the brochure. "Have you advertised in the newspaper before?" she asked.

"Yes. Last year, we ran a few ads in the "Professionals" section."

"How many customers did it bring in?" Vivian asked.

Becky frowned. "I don't really know; we weren't tracking that then. But I don't think very many."

"Well then let's concentrate on those media in which you know you have a good response," Vivian said. "You told me last week that your radio campaign two years ago did very well for you."

"We got lots of new customers. I know that because when people called, they asked about our 24-hour service and that was the first time we had advertised it."

Vivian put the brochure down on the desk. "Let's see if we can calculate your customer response from that campaign so that we can see if it's worth repeating."

We will ignore the impact of the time value of money for this example, but to be slightly more accurate, the total value would be a little less as tomorrow's dollars are not worth as much as today's dollars.

By this calculation, instead of this being a $40 customer, he or she is an almost $900 customer. NOW what would you spend to get this customer's business? Significantly more than $40.

Covering the Cost of the "Dry Holes"

Let's take the information that we have just learned about the lifetime value of a customer and tie it back into your growth plan.

Let's look at Janine's bottled-water company again. Janine has made some growth projections for the upcoming year. Her goal is to attract 30 new customers in the new year. We have seen that each of these new customers is worth $858.90 in profit to Janine over an average three-year period, so this translates into a three-year revenue increase of $25,767. Janine knows from experience that she can convert 65 percent of inquiries into sales. Therefore, she has calculated the required inquiries as:

30 new customers ÷ 65% = 46 inquiries

In other words, in order to reach her goal of 30 new customers next year, she needs to generate 46 inquiries through her marketing efforts. Therefore, Janine's marketing efforts have to cover the cost of 46 leads.

How would Janine know what kind of marketing effort it takes to generate 46 leads? She has tracked her former marketing campaigns. So, Janine knows, for example, that when she runs a display ad for three consecutive months in the local business magazine (at a cost of $2,250), it generates 16 leads on average. She also knows that when she runs a series of 48 radio spots (at a package cost of $7,350) during the morning drive time on the local talk radio station, it will bring in, on average, 39 calls. Janine's experience has shown her that when she runs advertising campaigns in multiple media (like print and radio), the lead generations for each go down by 10 percent as some inquiries would come in because potential customers were responding to both initiatives.

Combining the two advertising initiatives would bring in:

16 (print) + 39 (radio) - 10% = 49 leads

Janine has chosen to run both marketing initiatives simultaneously as it will generate slightly more than the 46 leads that she needs to get her 30 new customers. But is the cost worth the benefit?

Let's look at each one:

Cost

Print ads	**$2,250**
Radio	7,350
Total cost	**$9,600**

Benefit

30 customers X $858.90 =	**$25,767**

This tells Janine that the cost of the campaign of $9,600 is far less than the benefit she will receive of $25,767 over the average three-year lifetime of the new customers and, therefore, is beneficial for her to run.

Customers Beget Customers

The one happy complexity that we have not yet looked at is the fact that new customers will bring in more new customers. When customers are happy with your service or product, they will tell their friends and associates. In Janine's case (above), the 30 new customers that she is aiming for will most likely result in many more customers. Once you have had experience tracking your business growth, you will be able to incorporate growth due to referrals into your calculations.

This demonstrates the power of measuring and monitoring your business's historical performance. By doing so, you will be able to make marketing and growth decisions with more precision and with less cost. You will know which methods of attracting new customers work and which ones are doomed to fail. Without this knowledge, you will be doomed to repeat your failures at significant cost in time and money. Using the knowledge gives you a distinct advantage over your competitors.

Checklist 11
YOUR MARKETING AND PROMOTIONS

1. I have calculated the average lifetime value of my customer. ❑

2. I know how many leads I will have to generate to be able to attain my planned number of customers. ❑

3. I know what my historical track record has been regarding how many new customers each of my marketing initiatives has yielded. ❑

4. I have determined the optimal mix of advertising initiatives that will provide my business with the most profitable leads at the least cost. ❑

5. I have set the budget for advertising for the next 12 months. ❑

6. I have set up a plan to provide incentives to existing customers to refer new customers to my business. ❑

7. I have ensured that the advertising copy for the upcoming 12 months is in step with my company's vision and mission statements. ❑

Chapter Summary

➡ The lifetime value of a customer is simply the total amount of profit that the customer will add to your business for the length of time that the customer-supplier relationship lasts.

➡ The cost of your advertising and marketing has to cover the costs of the inquiries from people who will choose not to buy from you as well as the new customers.

➡ If the cost of an advertising campaign is less than the estimated benefit from net profit on new customers, the campaign is worth undertaking.

Chapter

28

Your People

Of all the difficult processes that you will learn as a small-business owner, human resource management may be the most challenging. Not only will you have to hire, train, and (unfortunately) fire employees, you will have to learn all about the applicable labor laws in your jurisdiction, as well as payroll withholdings and taxes. Not to mention how to keep your staff happy, motivated, and productive! Once you have more than just yourself and your immediate family working in your business, there are many added complexities. However, if you want to grow your business, ultimately you will have to leverage the labor of others.

How Do You Know When It's Time to Hire?

Most small businesses begin with one person: the owner/manager. If the business is successful, customer need will eventually outstrip the time that the owner/manager has available.

There are many indications that it's time for the business to hire an outside employee. However, before any hiring is done, it's critical to have all of the four foundation walls (as discussed in Chapter 17) in place. This means that, in addition to entrepreneurial drive and vision, you need to have an appropriate record keeping system, have a management operating plan in place, and know what your growth and expense projections are. Many small businesses make the mistake of hiring too early or too late because they didn't know what goals the business had and what it was looking for from a new employee.

Once you have the basics in place, there are several "road markers" that you can look out for that will tell you that it's time to start looking for an employee:

- Your revenues would increase by more than the additional payroll expense if you were able to concentrate on your strengths.

191

- You are unable to spend at least 20 percent of your time working *on* your business in the planning and strategizing activities.

- You do not have the time to implement the marketing and promotion plan that's required to achieve your projected growth.

- You are approaching your capacity with regards to labor inputs (i.e., your projected sales will require more hours than are physically possible).

- You are spending money on late fees and penalties because you cannot stay on top of the accounts payable and the required government filings.

- You begin to feel tired and "burned out" all of the time. You will notice the impact of this state fairly quickly as your productivity will decline drastically.

Any one of these indicators requires that you spend some time considering additional staff. Before you hire, however, you will have to decide what you need that person to do.

What Will a New Employee Do?

There are many different ways to decide what you want your new employee or employees to do. It could be that they look after the things that you're not getting around to doing, or the things that you're not very good at or that you don't like doing.

The first step in making that decision is to outline all the "jobs" in your business. You may not have thought about your business as having several different jobs because you are the only one doing them. It may all seem like one super-sized job to you. Separating out the functions, however, will help you to decide what needs to be done.

Jobs are simply a collection of processes. In previous chapters, we have changed, deleted, and added processes as we have built our business machine. These processes can be grouped into natural clusters to form an employee's job responsibilities. Some of the common processes are:

- Accounts receivable (billing, collection, tracking, cash handling)

- Accounts payable (tracking, check production)

- Office support (answering calls, greeting customers, booking appointments, filing, making coffee)

- Sales (customer presentations, follow-up, cold-calling, trade shows)

- Marketing and promotion (managing advertising, marketing tools design, writing copy, customer letters)

CASE STUDY

"I have to admit," Joe said, "I'm a little nervous about hiring a plumber's apprentice. What if we don't get along with each other? And what if he screws up a job? I can't look over his shoulder all the time."

Vivian said, "Some of those issues can be dealt with in the interview process. You'll be able to get a good idea about how he or she operates. You've already done the projections and you know that hiring someone skilled is essential to your growth plan."

"I know. We've just never had any experience with employees before. I don't know how to go about it."

Vivian said, "Let's start with the basics."

- Production (running the equipment, providing services to customers)
- Operations management (overseeing the production process, supervising employees, operational reporting)

Once you have outlined what the processes are in your business, it's time to document them. This will clarify for you and your employee what the expectations of the job are. Sample 16 is a sample documentation of the accounts receivable process in a small pest control company. You can modify and customize as you need to create your own template.

In a small business, this process likely would not take enough time to be a full job. It would be combined with other processes to form an employee's workload.

Once you have outlined all the processes in your business, take some time to honestly assess your own strengths and weaknesses. Are you good at sales but not so good at bookkeeping? Are you skilled at putting together a detailed budget but not at handling customer complaints? The goal here is to give yourself the set of processes where you add the most value, and hire someone to do a great job at the processes where you are the weakest.

Sample 16
DOCUMENTING YOUR WORK PROCESSES

BeGone Pest Control Inc.
Process Documentation

Process name: Accounts receivable

Process goals: To bill customers and collect monies owed in a timely manner. To minimize bad debts and to maximize customer good will.

Process tasks:

Bill customer for services rendered within one business day.

Send statements of account to all customers who have outstanding accounts at the end of every calendar month. Statements will be sent by the fifth of the following month.

Telephone all customers who have accounts outstanding for 45 days to request payment.

Send final notice statements of account to all customers who have outstanding accounts for 60 days.

Liaise with the collection agency regarding delinquent accounts.

Process receipts and update accounting system the day of the receipt.

The Laws of the Land

Now you know what skill set you are looking for. Great! But before you place that first ad for a new employee, it's important to understand your rights and responsibilities as an employer. These rules will be different in every jurisdiction so make sure that your information is correct. Call your local government office or speak with your accountant about it. This will save you considerable grief in the future.

Most jurisdictions have rules on the following topics:

- The type of workplace that you must provide for an employee

- The minimum wage you can pay

- How hazardous materials with which the employee comes into contact must be stored

- How much paid vacation time and sick days an employee is entitled to

- What deductions you must withhold from an employee's paycheck and remit to the government

- How maternity leaves are to be handled by the employer

- Under what circumstances you can fire an employee and how much notice he or she is to be given

There may be dozens of other rules that you must follow, so make sure you get a handle on them before hiring.

Attracting Quality Employees

Now you're ready to advertise for your first employee. You know what you want the employee to do and you know what skill set you are looking for. But how can you express that in an ad? And how do you make your ad more attractive to potential candidates than those of your competitors?

Your ad will have several considerations:

1. **The job description.** Have a clearly worded description so that candidates get a good sense right away what's involved in the job and whether they have the requisite skills.

2. **The business description.** Describe your business and its industry.

3. **The requirements.** Here's where you tell the candidates what they need to have in the way of education, experience, or technical skills. Be as clear as possible so that you do not have to wade through dozens of resumes with unsuitable qualifications.

4. **Contact information.** Describe how the candidates should respond to the ad: by telephone, fax, email, or in person. Including this information will save you from unwanted interruptions in your business day. It can also pick out unsuitable candidates right away. For example, if your ad states that potential candidates should fax their resume and three people show up in person, it tells you that these three might not be very good at following rules. In some positions, this might be a plus, but in most situations, this can be a negative quality.

5. **Tone.** The tone of your ad is difficult to quantify but it tells potential employees a lot about your business and the workplace environment. For example, if your environment is casual and laid back, you will want to convey that by using an informal tone in your ad, which will let candidates know up front whether or not that is the environment they want to work in.

Sample 17 is an actual employment ad that I ran in my own accounting firm.

Sample 17
EMPLOYMENT ADVERTISEMENT

Create Beans,
don't just count them!

If you want to be a key team member in a fast-paced, fun, and different kind of accounting firm, then we want to hear from you!

Our new Director of Compliance Services will have the following skills:

- The ability to provide top-notch client service
- Outstanding, proven leadership skills
- Experience in an accounting firm
- Above-average computer skills
- A positive, upbeat attitude

The **REWARDS** are many!

- Above-average compensation
- A dynamic, exciting work environment
- The ability to shape your own career
- A performance-based bonus structure

Please send resume along with cover letter to:

Mohr & Company
1111 Any Street
Anytown, Anyprovince T0T 0T0

Think of your ad as a way to present your business to highly skilled, motivated potential employees. Remember that your customers will also read your ad. They will get a strong sense of the quality of your staff from what you are asking for in the ad, so make sure that your ad exudes professionalism and demands the same from employees.

Once you have a number of resumes in front of you, it's time to narrow the playing field. Start by removing any candidate who does not have the background or skills asked for in the ad (I will guarantee that you will get some of those, especially in a tough job market). Have a look at the remaining resumes. Are there candidates who are clearly more qualified than others? Is there someone who claims to have outstanding attention to detail but who misspells several words in the cover letter? Is there someone with important skills that you did not even consider when placing the ad?

Narrow your field to a half dozen candidates or less. You will want to interview several people as you are also honing your hiring skills. You want as much experience as possible at the task.

The Interview

It's now time to talk to your potential candidates. There are many theories on the interview process, and it would be a good idea to pick up a good book on interviewing skills.

The purpose of the interview is for the candidate and the employer to find out enough information to assess whether this would be a good job fit. Never forget that the candidate will be interviewing you too. Ensure that you are prepared and professional — the same qualities you are looking for in an employee.

It's best to have your interview questions prepared ahead of time. That way, you'll know that you've asked everything you meant to and you will be able to compare answers among candidates.

During the interview, talk to the candidate about your business. Tell him or her about how you've systematized processes and about your growth plans for the future. An appropriate candidate will be interested in learning more about your business.

Ultimately, you will make your decision based on a combination of factors, including the answers to your questions, professional image, enthusiasm, salary expectations, and "gut feel." As you become more experienced in human resource management, your instincts will be sharper and more valuable to you.

Hiring from an Employment Agency

With strict labor laws in most industrialized countries, it can be very difficult to let an employee go once he or she has been hired on a permanent basis. There is also great expense to the employer of hiring and training an employee who doesn't work out, never mind the stress of firing someone.

That's why many employers hire temporary employees and it can be a valuable strategy for small-business owners. Many employment agencies hire out workers on a weekly or monthly basis to businesses that have variable staffing needs. For example, if your busy time is at Christmas and you need help to fill orders over the holiday season, you may wish to hire someone on a temporary basis. At the end of the contract, the employee goes back to the agency to be hired by some other business.

Hiring a temporary employee has some benefits for you if you are hiring your first employee:

- The agency has already performed much of the pre-screening.

- You will get a better sense of what you are looking for in an employee once you have one.

- If the person doesn't work out or you find out that you don't have enough work to keep him or her busy, you can send the employee back to the agency at the end of the contract, without the challenges surrounding firing a permanent employee.

- If the employee and your business end up being a match made in heaven, you can hire the employee on a permanent basis. (The agency may have some rules about that, so make sure you find out what they are ahead of time).

- Hiring a temporary employee can be a great way to "get your feet wet" in the human resource area.

Goal-Based Compensation

Once you have gotten through the jungle of defining roles, advertising, interviewing, and hiring a new employee, you may think that it's time to put your feet up and take a breather. But not so! (You knew I was going to say that.) A more difficult challenge than hiring a great employee is keeping a great employee. Lots of businesses are looking for skilled labor. You are in competition not only with other businesses in your industry but with all other businesses in your area. Savvy workers will continually be looking for better opportunities with more pay and greater benefits. It is your responsibility to make sure not only that the employee is a good fit with your business, but also that he or she is motivated and happy to come to work everyday. These are skills that you need to learn to be successful, but which are outside the scope of this book.

One valuable facet of managing employees is to make sure that they are compensated to do the things that you want them to do. This ensures that the performance of the employees is in sync with the goals of your business. For example, if employees have control over the sales function, make part of their compensation based on sales growth, not expense reduction. Reward them for furthering the vision of the business and let them participate in the strategic outlook.

So Long, Farewell, Auf Wiedersehen, Adieu

One of the hardest tasks you will ever perform as an employer is to have to fire someone. Not only is it disruptive from an operations standpoint, but it also has implications on personal relationships and finances. How would you feel if you had to fire a single mother and remove her only source of income?

The best way to avoid this is to spend considerable time and effort in the hiring process. It's also critical to give feedback in the employee evaluation process so that you are both "on the same page" regarding expectations and obstacles. Sometimes, however, an employment situation just doesn't work out no matter how hard both parties have tried. How do you know it's time to let someone go? Here are some signs:

- Negative customer feedback

- Tension with other employees

- A significant reduction in productivity

- Inability to complete job functions without constant supervision and prodding

- Declining morale in the office

Any one of these signs can be due to a number of factors, so it is only after you have

CASE STUDY

Becky shuffled through the pile of resumes and looked up at Vivian. "Well, we got 17 resumes and we interviewed 5 candidates."

Vivian asked, "And did you and Joe come to a decision?"

"Yeah," Joe said. "We both agreed on Martin. Before we interviewed him, I didn't think that he'd be the one. But he's got all the skills and he's worked for a plumber before, so he's got experience. And he seems easy to get along with."

"Now we just have to keep him!" Becky said.

discussed the problems with the employee and have given him or her an opportunity to fix them that you should consider termination. You will also have to be familiar with employment law in your jurisdiction so that you do not end up looking at the business end of a wrongful termination lawsuit.

There are costs involved in hiring, training, supervising, and firing employees. How you handle these activities can have an impact on your bottom line, so take the time to do it right.

Checklist 12
YOUR PEOPLE

1. I have calculated whether my projected increase in revenues from hiring an employee will outweigh the cost. ☐

2. I have reviewed whether I am still able to spend at least 20 percent of my working time on planning and strategizing activities. ☐

3. I have outlined all the jobs in my business. ☐

4. I have clustered all the jobs in my business into natural clusters to form employees' job responsibilities. ☐

5. I have prepared complete documentation for every procedure in the business. ☐

6. I have educated myself regarding the employment laws in my jurisdiction. ☐

7. I have written an employment ad that encompasses not only the specific job responsibilities, but also the nature of the working environment. ☐

8. I have considered hiring a temporary employee. ☐

9. I have documented the employment contract and the basis of compensation. ☐

Chapter Summary

➡ You'll know it's time to hire an employee when the increased revenues due to having an employee more than offset the increased payroll expense, allowing you to focus on your strengths.

➡ Have a detailed description of all your internal processes and an accurate assessment of your own strengths and weaknesses before you decide what skills and background you require from potential candidates.

➡ It may be beneficial to hire on a temporary basis your first time to get a better idea of what you're really looking for.

➡ Waiting too long to fire someone who is a bad fit can have serious repercussions on the morale of the business.

Chapter

29

Your Systems

So far, we have looked at making changes in our business in order to grow successfully: changes in our marketing approach, our human resource policies, and the way we interact with customers.

Now it's time to bring all of the new ways of doing things together to make a cohesive guidebook for your business.

The Goals of Systemization

The goal of growing your business is to increase profits and ultimately increase the value of the business in order to sell it. The reason a systems

approach works is that it allows you, the owner and manager of the business, to repeat processes and procedures in a predictable and consistent way. It also allows you to train your staff to perform these functions exactly the same way that you would. Not only does this give customers a consistent buying experience, but it also makes it easier for staff to learn new tasks and feel confident that they are doing things the right way (i.e., the way you want them to do it).

In the second book in the *Numbers 101 for Small Business* series, *Financial Management 101*,

---

CASE STUDY

"It's hard to believe that everything we do is in that binder," Becky said, leafing through the new Joe's Plumbing procedures manual.

Joe added, "Yeah. It's not so long ago that we didn't even know what we were doing, never mind being able to write it down in a way that makes sense."

"It makes our company feel more permanent somehow. Like it's going to outlast us," said Becky.

"The real test will come soon when the new apprentice reads it over. Then we'll know whether it makes sense to anyone else."

we learned how to develop a management operating plan. This is a tool for you as the owner and manager of your business to track critical business processes such as the following topics:

- Team meeting agendas and minutes
- Key performance indicators
- Historical financial statements
- Budgets and cash flow projections

Documentation of your systems will form a part of this management operating plan. In my accounting firm, we called this, "How We Do It Here," which is pretty self-explanatory.

"How We Do It Here"

Your process and procedure manual (whatever you choose to call it) should start with your business's vision and mission statements. These are the first things a new employee needs to know about your business: its guiding principles and focus. The principles in the vision and mission statements form the underlying basis for every procedure and every customer interaction.

Knowing these principles will also allow employees to identify areas where the procedures do not further the goals of the organization. In this way, the employees will ensure that the manual is continually reviewed and fine-tuned.

After the vision and mission statements, include a section on your human resource policy. There will be many parts to this (an example follows in Sample 18 at the end of this chapter). In this section, you will cover the following issues:

- Hours of work
- Vacation and sick leave
- Dress code
- Overtime policy
- Performance evaluation process
- Reporting structure

There may be other issues important to your business that you wish to include. The purpose of this section is to give employees a clear sense of your expectations of them. This will serve you well as it provides an objective starting point from which to discuss any performance problems in the future.

Following the human resource section, you can include your procedure documentation, grouped by process. For example, in your marketing section (a process), you might have a sheet for advertising policies, one for trade show procedures, and one for how referrals are generated and handled.

The procedural documentation should be specific and clear. To test that this is the case, have a new employee read the documentation

---

CASE STUDY

"That's the most detailed "how to" guide I've ever seen," said Martin. "Everything's in here. Why we do things, how to do them, everything."

Becky said, "Take some time to read it over carefully. We've put a lot of effort into creating systems for this company so that it will run more smoothly."

Martin said, "Well, I look forward to working here. You're certainly a lot more organized than the last place I worked."

Joe and Becky laughed and smiled at each other, remembering the not too distant past where organization didn't even seem possible.

for a particular procedure and see if he or she can perform the task based on the manual. Anything that you have to explain should be incorporated into the documentation. The goal is to make training easy and consistent, with a minimum amount of your time.

Continuous Improvement

Like all areas of your business, the systems you develop will be constantly refined, tested, and fine-tuned.

For example, you may have discovered that the telephone script you are currently using converts 62 percent of inquiries into sales. Test a new script to see if does better. Change the headlines that you use in your print advertising and test whether the new one generates more leads than the old one. By making sure that your business is fresh and growing, you can help defer the decline stage of your business's life cycle.

As new processes are developed and old ones become obsolete, make sure that you update your operations manual. If you have employees, assign the updating responsibility to one of them. That will ensure that it actually gets done.

Developing and refining the systems in your business will set you apart from your competitors. Take the time to do it right!

Sample 18 is an excerpt from the policy manual from my own company. You can use it as a starting point for developing your own policy manual to document your systems approach.

HUMAN RESOURCE POLICY

(Excerpt from the Mohr & Company policy manual)

HOW WE DO IT HERE
Our Team's Commitment to Each Other

1. Each team member will treat other team members with respect and professionalism.

2. Team members will ensure that any concerns or issues they may have are raised with the appropriate person or the managing partner.

3. All team members deserve to know how they are performing and semi-annual performance appraisal reviews (PARS) will be held with each team member and his or her manager. Input on performance will be solicited from all members of the team.

4. Each team member plays an integral role in the success of the firm. Therefore, every person has a responsibility to provide input on making the team and the firm better. All suggestions and recommendations will be taken seriously by all team members and discussed.

5. Each team member should realize that the goal of the firm is to get all work done in a timely manner. Team members should recognize situations where they might be able to help another team member with a task, and the team should discuss resource allocation of the firm as a whole.

Working Hours

The office is generally open from 9 until 5 Monday to Friday and there must be at least one staff member present in the office at all times. Keeping this general rule in mind, team members may exercise their own judgment in planning their working hours, remembering that the needs of the clients supersede this flexibility.

Our standard work week is 37.5 hours and any hours worked in excess of the standard can be "banked" and used as time off in the future.

Employees will receive two weeks of paid vacation, the timing of which will be discussed and approved by the entire team.

Sample 18 — Continued

Employees will be paid for a maximum of six sick days during a calendar year. Any sick days in excess of this will be deducted from the team member's pay. Family emergencies (the illness of a child, for example) can be taken as part of the paid sick leave.

Internet and Email Use Policy

The internet and email access is primarily for company use. Uses of Internet and email include accounting and tax research, downloading of government forms, and correspondence with clients and other team members.

It is understood that some personal transactions are most easily handled on the Internet, such as web banking. These types of personal uses are acceptable as long as the time taken is minimal. Excessive Internet browsing for personal purposes should be done at home.

Under no circumstances should any information or document of any kind be downloaded from the internet unless approved by the partners. Downloading can expose the network to malicious viruses. The partners can provide you with a list of "safe" websites from which it is low risk to download information.

Your email address, yourname@mohrandcompany.com, exists for the purpose of contacting and conversing with clients and team members. Personal email should not be sent or received from this email address. You may wish to set up a free email account through MSN®, Yahoo!®, etc., for the purpose of personal correspondence, and you may check this account periodically as per the Internet use rules above.

Dress Code

All team members should dress professionally at the office. The dress code is "business casual." For men, this means well-pressed pants and either a dress shirt or golf shirt. For women, this means a well-pressed skirt or pants and a blouse, dress shirt, or golf shirt.

As an alternative, team members can wear tan or black dress pants and shirts with the company logo.

Team members should be aware that there may be times when more formal dress is appropriate.

Checklist 13
YOUR SYSTEMS

1. I have reviewed all processes and procedures in my business to make sure that they are efficient and relevant. ☐

2. I have prepared a complete process and procedure manual for my company on planning and strategizing activities. ☐

3. I have prepared a training and professional development program for all my employees. ☐

4. All my employees have read the company's vision and mission statements and understand them. ☐

5. All my employees are thoroughly trained on all their job responsibilities. ☐

6. All my employees have read and understand the company's human resource policies. ☐

7. I have set up a system to continuously monitor and measure my company's systems. ☐

Chapter Summary

➡ Having systems in your business allows you and your employees to operate in a repeatable, consistent fashion.

➡ Having a process and procedures manual as part of your monthly operating plan conveys "the way we do it here" to all employees, which gives you greater freedom from having to supervise.

➡ A process and procedures manual contains documentation on the business's vision and mission statements, human resource policies, and operational procedures.

➡ Systems should be frequently revised and tested to continuously improve your business, and the procedures manual should be updated to reflect any changes.

Business Acquisitions

So far in this book, we have discussed growing your business organically, by building a customer base from the ground up and using customer attraction and retention strategies.

There is another method of growth, however: Buying customers. This can be accomplished in one of three ways:

- Buying a group of customers from another business

- Buying a business solely for its customer list

- Buying a business to run separately from your existing business

Regardless of which method you use, there are several issues to be considered when buying customers, including quality assessment, valuation, and infrastructure changes. Growing your business by purchasing another business can give you instant rewards, but only if managed in a planned, consistent way.

Another Way to Grow

There are many reasons why you might choose to purchase a business rather than develop your own customer base. These may include:

- High initial investment in capital equipment or staff. In some businesses that use specialized equipment in the manufacturing process, the high up-front investment needs to be recovered quickly in order to stay afloat. In this situation, it would make sense to build the customer base as quickly as possible to reach capacity in order to offset the high fixed costs. An example would be a print shop. The printing and lithography equipment is quite expensive so it would make sense to purchase the customers of another print shop to generate revenues quickly.

- Low barriers for "copycat" competitors. Sometimes, being the first out of the gate ensures that your business will be successful. Therefore, you need a full customer roster before other businesses get the same idea. An example would be if an entrepreneur opens the first paralegal service in town. Competitors would quickly see the benefits of starting up this type of company, so it makes sense for the entrepreneur to quickly ramp up to capacity (i.e., have lots of customers) before the competition get wind of the new business and try to build a customer base of their own.

- A desire to step into a successful turnkey system. Some entrepreneurs want to take advantage of a system that is guaranteed to work because the business has a great track record (remember that this is also how you want potential purchasers to feel about your business someday).

- The ability to sell to the new block of customers your complementary service or product. You may have a product or service that would almost automatically sell to a group of customers. For example, if you purchase a hairdressing salon, there's a good chance that those customers would be very interested in the spa services that your business provides (and vice versa).

What Are You Buying?

So how can you tell if a potential business acquisition is a good idea?

First, make sure you understand what you are purchasing. There are two main ways of buying a business: Asset purchase and share purchase. Each has its own considerations. It is critical that you engage the services of an experienced lawyer and accountant before negotiating any business acquisition.

As well, when you buy the shares of a business, you are also buying its goodwill and customer lists.

Asset purchase

In an asset purchase, you are only buying certain assets of the business. In most situations, you will not be responsible for the debts or dealings that the business engaged in prior to the purchase. For example, you may be purchasing equipment, raw materials, inventory, or a customer list.

In some situations, you may be purchasing the net assets of the business, which means that you will be assuming responsibility for the liabilities as well. In this case, you would need to obtain legal comfort regarding the extent and terms of the liabilities. You wouldn't want, for example, to purchase the net assets of a business only to find out later that the equipment loan is due in 30 days and is $10,000 more than you thought.

Share purchase

You may also purchase the shares of a business. This basically transfers the rights and responsibilities of the ownership of the business from the seller to you. You would now own everything that the business owns, including assets, corporate information, and the business names and logos.

You would also have complete liability for the past dealings of the business, including any lawsuits, warranties, or debts as well as any back taxes owing to the government. Some of this liability can be reduced or removed through provisions in the purchase contract. You might include a clause that says that you can seek compensation from the seller for any former liabilities. This would still leave you in a position to have to settle up first and try to recover later, which could seriously disrupt your operations and cash flow.

There are, however, some benefits to purchasing the entire business through a share purchase. There are tax benefits in many jurisdictions, but, more important, you own all the goodwill that the former business has generated, as well as the business's current customer list.

Goodwill

When you buy a business, you are also buying its goodwill. Goodwill is difficult to pin down. It is an asset of the business (sometimes the most important one) but it does not have substance like manufacturing equipment or desks or raw materials. There are many accounting and legal definitions, but we are speaking here in the general sense of the word. Goodwill refers to the ability of the business to attract and retain customers. You can also define it as the business's reputation. That reputation might have been built on many platforms, which can include:

- High community profile
- Charitable donations
- Customer service
- Quality of product or service
- Treatment of employees

Buying goodwill can be a huge benefit to you as customers will come to see you because of the former activities of the business. Of course, you can always destroy that goodwill by operating the business differently than the previous owners.

In most purchase situations where the business involved has built up goodwill, the purchase price will reflect that. Therefore, the cost to you will generally be more than the value of the hard assets (we will discuss valuation later on in the chapter).

Customer lists

A customer list is almost as difficult to define as goodwill. You can't touch it or see it, but it is a valuable asset, nonetheless. A customer list simply refers to the database of current and former customer names, addresses, and other contact information. The value of a customer list lies in marketing. It is always easier and less expensive to market to an existing customer than to attract a new customer.

For example, if you are considering purchasing a bed and breakfast in Vermont, you would (all other things being equal) be willing to pay more for one that has tracked its customers over the years and knows who they are and how many times they have stayed in the bed and breakfast. Having this information would allow you to send letters to these former guests, updating them on the happenings of the bed and breakfast and offering them special discounts or packages.

In Chapter 22, we looked at the importance of tracking customers and their buying patterns. These same principles apply to purchasing a business; it's worth more if you have a marketable customer base.

Valuing the Acquisition

Business valuation lies somewhere between a science and an art. There are dozens of books on the subject and several professional designations. The theory and application of business valuation is beyond the scope of this book, but we can look at some general considerations and some parameters.

What would you pay to buy a business? Well, the least amount that the business is worth is the liquidation value of its net assets. Let's look at a potential business purchase example. The business is a bed and breakfast, a century home in a tourist district where people can book rooms that entitle them to breakfast the next morning. The business has provided you with the information outlined in Sample 19.

How much would you pay for this business? That may be a difficult and subjective decision but at least we can put some parameters around it.

Floor price

Floor price means the absolute minimum that we would pay for the business. If we look at it from a common sense perspective, we could buy the business today and sell the assets and settle the liabilities tomorrow.

Therefore, the least that the business is worth is the fair market value of its hard assets (i.e., those that you can see or touch) minus the settlement value of the liabilities. In this case, the total market value of the assets is $380,985. From that amount, we would have to settle up total liabilities of $303,599, leaving us with $77,386 in our pockets. Therefore, we would at least be willing to pay $77,386 for the business because we know that we can easily get that back out of the business.

Sample 19
VALUING A BUSINESS ACQUISITION

PARADISE GARDENS B&B FINANCIAL INFORMATION

Assets: Fair market value (FMV)

House and land	$347,000
Furnishings	29,350
In-house equipment (fridge/stove/washer/dryer)	3,210
Outside equipment (lawn mower/tiller/hand tools)	1,425

Liabilities

Mortgage	$276,349
Line of credit	23,000
Property taxes in arrears	4,250

Other information

- B&B has maintained an 80 percent occupancy rate for the past six years.
- Fully rented, the B&B generates $93,075 from its three rooms.
- Operating expenses (including one maid) average $57,215 annually.
- 75 percent of customers have booked a room more than once.

But we also know that the fact that we already have a steady stream of customers is worth something as well. It won't take much effort on our part to maintain the 80 percent occupancy rate. The business already has made a name for itself and people are willing to come back time and time again. We're not starting this business with three empty rooms that we quickly need to fill if we're going to cover our fixed costs.

We know that, if we experience the same occupancy rate and the same operating expenses as the former owners, we will make $17,245 annually right out of the gate. So, in a sense, on top of purchasing the net assets of the business, we are also purchasing a stream of profit. The art and science of business valuation is to determine how much that stream of profit is worth to a purchaser.

Ceiling price

The ceiling price refers to the maximum we would pay for a business. In this case, we know that it will be more than the $77,386 floor price.

It will be important to make sure that we can recover our investment in a reasonable time frame. For example, if we pay $100,000 for this business, it will take almost six years to achieve payback. This may or may not be a reasonable amount of time depending on your goals and income requirements.

The payback concept becomes more critical when evaluating your options.

Evaluating the Choices

If you have the option of choosing among several purchase possibilities, you need to choose one that best meets your goals. Earlier in the chapter, we talked about the reasons entrepreneurs buy a business, and some of the intangible benefits may well come into play in your decision.

From a strictly numbers standpoint, the best choice is the business that generates the most profit for the least investment. For example, if two businesses cost $50,000 each to buy and one generates $10,000 in profit annually and the other generates $14,000, clearly the second option provides the higher profit for the same money (a "bigger bang for the buck," so to speak).

On top of this basic decision model, however, you will have to factor in what other financial benefits you will receive from each purchase. If one of the businesses has customers to whom you can sell your existing products, this will be a better choice than a business that will stand alone and with which there will not be any opportunity to cross sell.

With the help of your business advisors, you'll need to weigh the financial pros and cons of each choice against each other to determine which is the better buy.

Checklist 14
BUSINESS ACQUISITIONS

1. I have investigated the possibility and attractiveness of purchasing a group of customers from another business. ☐

2. I have investigated the possibility and attractiveness of buying another business solely for its customer list. ☐

3. I have investigated the possibility and attractiveness of buying another business to run in addition to my current business. ☐

4. I have investigated all of the costs and benefits of purchasing a company's shares versus buying its assets. ☐

5. I can calculate the value of a business's goodwill. ☐

6. I know how to calculate a basic valuation range for a potential business acquisition. ☐

7. I know what the comparative risks are for each of my potential purchases. ☐

Chapter Summary

➡ Buying a business rather than growing one from scratch can offer several benefits, including an immediate profit stream, a recognizable brand name, or a marketable customer list.

➡ You can buy a business by either buying the assets of the business or by buying shares.

➡ Buying shares allows you to retain the goodwill that the business has built over time.

➡ In order to evaluate and value a potential business purchase, you need to weigh all of the financial advantages you will generate from the purchase.

Chapter 31

Exit Strategies

It may seem very strange to you to be thinking about leaving your business when you put so much effort into starting it up and growing it. But there will come a time when you will want to move on, and the earlier you plan for that eventuality, the better off you will be. Even if you plan on working until you drop, you will indeed drop someday and you need to have planned out what happens to the business then.

Many exit strategies require months or years to implement, so it makes sense to map out the strategy that's best for you as early as possible.

Your Personal Goals

In Chapter 21, we looked at your business goals in order to put together a growth plan. Now we need to review your personal goals. Ask yourself: What do you want to do after running your business?

The answers to that question are as unique as each entrepreneur. You may decide that there's nothing more appealing than lying on a faraway beach sipping margaritas. You may want to start another business, perhaps in a different industry. You may choose to mentor young entrepreneurs as they face the same pitfalls you have over the years. It's important to define your goals because they will affect how you will transfer your business and how you will structure payments.

Heading for the Exits

There are many ways to transfer your business to others. Let's look at the most common.

Passing on the business to your children

One common way to transfer your business is to pass it on to your children, which is also

217

known as succession planning. Many small-business owners want to keep the business empire that they have created in the family to provide their children (or grandchildren) with a secure source of income. However, this form of selling the business can be the most difficult.

The first decision that has to be made is whether your children are truly interested in owning the business. Many small business owners get quite the shock to find out that their kids really don't want all the hassles of running a business. Even if they do want to take over the reins, they must go through the same decision process as you did when you started your business: defining business and personal goals, outlining a vision, and setting a growth plan.

A decision that you as the business owner must make is to define what is acceptable to you in how the business is run in the future. What if your children have a very different vision of the business and make substantial changes? Will you be comfortable with that? The more thought put into this type of succession up-front, the more likely the transition will be successful.

Selling the business to an outside party

If you don't have a family member who wants to take on the business, you may choose to sell your business to someone outside your family. It might be an employee, a competitor, or someone who wishes to purchase an existing business rather than start one from scratch (in which case, they will assess your business in the ways we discussed in Chapter 30).

It is more difficult to sell a business than you might think. That's why it's critical to plan ahead so that you can make sure that your business looks great on paper, is growing consistently, and will be attractive to potential buyers.

Brokers are frequently used in this type of sale. A broker's job is to match up buyers and sellers of businesses, much like a real estate broker's job is to match up buyers and sellers of houses. A broker may bring potential purchasers to the table whom you may not have otherwise met.

When selling to an outside buyer, timing is important. Ideally, you will want to sell your business when the economy is hot, your business's performance looks outstanding, and its reputation is stellar. The worst thing that you can do as a small business owner is to run your business until you can't stand it for another five minutes and then try to dump it for whatever you can get. You'll maximize the business's value (and price tag) if you sell when things are looking up rather than down.

Liquidating your business

If you have built a business that is completely dependent upon you and have not systematized your operations, liquidation of the business is probably your only option. Liquidation involves selling off the assets of the business and using those funds to pay the liabilities, which will only work if there are more assets in the business than liabilities. If the situation is reversed (i.e., there are more liabilities than assets), you may have to declare bankruptcy in order to get out of your business, otherwise you will have to continue to run it until the liabilities are paid.

The benefit of liquidation is that it tends to be easier than selling a business as a going concern. There are more potential buyers for individual assets than for an entire operation. The down side (and it's a big one!) is that you will almost always end up with less cash in your pocket at the end of the day by liquidating. There are two reasons for this:

- Equipment and other assets are generally valued higher if they are part of a continuing business.
- It is impossible to sell the goodwill of your business if you are liquidating.

Generally, liquidation is the least favorable option for you to pursue.

What's My Business Worth?

In Chapter 30, we talked about business valuation from the perspective of you, the buyer. All of those issues apply here when you are looking to put a price tag on your business. You know that your business is worth at least the fair market value of the assets minus the payout value of the liabilities. If you have been working to systematize and grow your business, it will be worth substantially more.

It is worth discussing your particular situation with a business valuator. (Your accountant or lawyer should be able to recommend one.) Undervaluing your business can have serious consequences on your retirement lifestyle, so it pays to do your homework and get professional help.

Getting Ready for the Sale

There are many things that you will have to do before putting any exit strategy in place, especially if you will be selling to outside buyers.

The first thing is to assemble your team of experts. This will most likely include your accountant, lawyer, financial planner, and perhaps a business valuator and broker. Make sure that all parties know your goals for the buyout and that they are all working in tandem to meet those goals.

Your accountant will help you steer through all your choices surrounding how to structure the sale and how to take payment. There will be practical decisions as well as taxation implications.

Your lawyer will help you structure the legal side of the sale and will help you interpret offers as they come in.

Your financial planner will look at your post-business goals and will help you determine what income level you will need in order to maintain your desired lifestyle (margaritas can get expensive!). We've already discussed the roles of the business valuator and the broker. They can be integral parts of your team.

Your accountant will most likely recommend that you prepare some financial information for the pending sale. Much like a real estate broker would suggest to you that you put a fresh coat of paint on your house and maybe plant some flowers outside before bringing buyers through, your accountant will recommend that you show potential buyers of your business what it might look like once they take over. You will have run your business in a way that suited you. You may have had the goal of minimizing tax or employing your family. These decisions might not be made the same way by the new owner.

Your accountant will get you to normalize your financial statements; in other words, recast them without all of the discretionary activity. If your spouse is on the payroll, remove the expense related to that. If you pay yourself high dividends, restate the financials without them. Keep in mind, however, that you need to be upfront with potential buyers about the changes you have made and how those statements differ from ones you have prepared for taxation purposes.

The Mechanics of the Sale

A sale can happen in one of two basic ways:
- Through the sale of assets
- Through the sale of shares

If your business is unincorporated, you will be selling the assets of the business. The buyer may choose to take on some or all of the business's liabilities rather than coming up with a lot of cash upfront. Your lawyer will ensure that your name is removed from those liabilities so that creditors cannot come after you later if the new owner stops paying them.

If you own a corporation, you can either sell the assets of the business or the shares of the corporation. Each has its own tax consequences and your accountant will help you weigh the pros and cons of each. If you are passing on your business to your children, there are many sophisticated ways to transfer shares and your accountant will advise you on the various methods. You may choose to structure the arrangement, for example, so that you are still a shareholder (albeit one who no longer works in the business) and will receive a monthly income for the rest of your life in the form of dividends.

Once you and a buyer agree on the nature of the sale, you must decide how you will receive the funds: either all upfront or over time.

Again, tax considerations come in to play here, but you must also consider the risk of financing part of the sale. If, for example, you agree to receive $50,000 upfront and $5,000 a month for 12 months, you are betting the farm on the fact that the new owner will still be in business a year from now. What if he or she runs the business into the ground? Or declares bankruptcy? You will lose some or all of the sales proceeds and may find yourself having to start up another business rather than lying on the beach. Your lawyer can help mitigate some of that risk through the structuring of the agreement.

Once the business has been sold, financial planning becomes a key issue, especially if you plan to retire. You are now dealing with a fixed amount of funds (which can grow through prudent investing) and you and your financial planner will have to make sure those funds plus your other sources of savings will last you for the rest of your life.

Checklist 15
EXIT STRATEGIES

1. I know what my retirement goals are. ❏

2. I have determined the time frame in which I want to retire. ❏

3. I have looked into the possibility of passing the business on to my heirs. ❏

4. I have considered the possibility of selling the business to an employee. ❏

5. I have looked into the opportunities for selling the business to an outside party. ❏

6. I have assessed the benefits and costs of simply liquidating the company. ❏

7. I have met with my accountant to prepare for the eventual sale of my business. ❏

Chapter Summary

➡ It's critical to set up your exit strategy early to make sure that you will ultimately harvest the most value from the business.

➡ You may choose to pass your business onto the next generation, sell it to a third party, or sell off the assets and wind up operations.

➡ The timing of the sale can have a significant impact on the price you ultimately receive.

➡ If your business is a corporation, you can either sell the assets of the business or sell the shares of the corporation.

Chapter

32

What Happens Next?

You've started a business, systematized its operations, and have grown it into a strong, successful, and lucrative company. The business now runs almost by itself with little intervention from you. You frequently entertain unsolicited offers to buy your business, but you're not quite ready to cash out yet. It takes less and less time to manage the business, even as it grows larger. What will you do with your extra time?

To answer that question, you need to go back to examine your personal and business goals, which may have changed over the years as you get a more developed sense of who you are. There are many things you can do with that free time:

- **Relax.** You may decide that you only want to work part time while you pursue hobbies (or those margaritas!).

- **Work in the business.** You may truly enjoy doing what the business does.

For example, if you own a law firm, you may really like trying cases. If so, feel free to do that, knowing that you've set up the machine to work on its own.

- **Start another business.** You may choose to go back to the beginning and start up a new business with all of the knowledge and experience you have gained over the years. You now know what it takes to be successful and you can avoid many of the pitfalls that may have snagged you the first time around.

- **Buy and sell businesses.** Another option (if you really enjoyed systematizing and building your business) is to purchase other businesses, fix them up to increase their value, and sell them for a profit. It's sort of like flipping houses. There are many entrepreneurs who have made their fortunes this way.

223

A Last Word

Owning a successful business has been the dream of entrepreneurs for centuries.

It's as much to do with designing your own destiny and securing your future as it is to do with the money. It takes a lot of work and planning to create a successful business, but the rewards are certainly worth it. May you always have great happiness and success!

Please feel free to email me at angie@numbers101.com to let me know how your business is doing.

Present Value of $1

PRESENT VALUE OF $1

PV TABLE

Discount Rate Period	1%	2%	3%	4%	5%	6%	7%	8%	9%	10%	12%	14%	16%	18%	20%	25%
1	0.9901	0.9804	0.9709	0.9615	0.9524	0.9434	0.9346	0.9259	0.9174	0.9091	0.8929	0.8772	0.8621	0.8475	0.8333	0.8000
2	0.9803	0.9612	0.9426	0.9246	0.9070	0.8900	0.8734	0.8573	0.8417	0.8264	0.7972	0.7695	0.7432	0.7182	0.6944	0.6400
3	0.9706	0.9423	0.9151	0.8890	0.8638	0.8396	0.8163	0.7938	0.7722	0.7513	0.7118	0.6750	0.6407	0.6086	0.5787	0.5120
4	0.9610	0.9238	0.8885	0.8548	0.8227	0.7921	0.7629	0.7350	0.7084	0.6830	0.6355	0.5921	0.5523	0.5158	0.4823	0.4096
5	0.9515	0.9057	0.8626	0.8219	0.7835	0.7473	0.7130	0.6806	0.6499	0.6209	0.5674	0.5194	0.4761	0.4371	0.4019	0.3277
6	0.9420	0.8880	0.8375	0.7903	0.7462	0.7050	0.6663	0.6302	0.5963	0.5645	0.5066	0.4556	0.4104	0.3704	0.3349	0.2621
7	0.9327	0.8706	0.8131	0.7599	0.7107	0.6651	0.6227	0.5835	0.5470	0.5132	0.4523	0.3996	0.3538	0.3139	0.2791	0.2097
8	0.9235	0.8535	0.7894	0.7307	0.6768	0.6274	0.5820	0.5403	0.5019	0.4665	0.4039	0.3506	0.3050	0.2660	0.2326	0.1678
9	0.9143	0.8368	0.7664	0.7026	0.6446	0.5919	0.5439	0.5002	0.4604	0.4241	0.3606	0.3075	0.2630	0.2255	0.1938	0.1342
10	0.9053	0.8203	0.7441	0.6756	0.6139	0.5584	0.5083	0.4632	0.4224	0.3855	0.3220	0.2697	0.2267	0.1911	0.1615	0.1074
11	0.8963	0.8043	0.7224	0.6496	0.5847	0.5268	0.4751	0.4289	0.3875	0.3505	0.2875	0.2366	0.1954	0.1619	0.1346	0.0859
12	0.8874	0.7885	0.7014	0.6246	0.5568	0.4970	0.4440	0.3971	0.3555	0.3186	0.2567	0.2076	0.1685	0.1372	0.1122	0.0687
13	0.8787	0.7730	0.6810	0.6006	0.5303	0.4688	0.4150	0.3677	0.3262	0.2897	0.2292	0.1821	0.1452	0.1163	0.0935	0.0550
14	0.8700	0.7579	0.6611	0.5775	0.5051	0.4423	0.3878	0.3405	0.2992	0.2633	0.2046	0.1597	0.1252	0.0985	0.0779	0.0440
15	0.8613	0.7430	0.6419	0.5553	0.4810	0.4173	0.3624	0.3152	0.2745	0.2394	0.1827	0.1401	0.1079	0.0835	0.0649	0.0352
16	0.8528	0.7284	0.6232	0.5339	0.4581	0.3936	0.3387	0.2919	0.2519	0.2176	0.1631	0.1229	0.0930	0.0708	0.0541	0.0281
17	0.8444	0.7142	0.6050	0.5134	0.4363	0.3714	0.3166	0.2703	0.2311	0.1978	0.1456	0.1078	0.0802	0.0600	0.0451	0.0225
18	0.8360	0.7002	0.5874	0.4936	0.4155	0.3503	0.2959	0.2502	0.2120	0.1799	0.1300	0.0946	0.0691	0.0508	0.0376	0.0180
19	0.8277	0.6864	0.5703	0.4746	0.3957	0.3305	0.2765	0.2317	0.1945	0.1635	0.1161	0.0829	0.0596	0.0431	0.0313	0.0144
20	0.8195	0.6730	0.5537	0.4564	0.3769	0.3118	0.2584	0.2145	0.1784	0.1486	0.1037	0.0728	0.0514	0.0365	0.0261	0.0115
21	0.8114	0.6598	0.5375	0.4388	0.3589	0.2942	0.2415	0.1987	0.1637	0.1351	0.0926	0.0638	0.0443	0.0309	0.0217	0.0092
22	0.8034	0.6468	0.5219	0.4220	0.3418	0.2775	0.2257	0.1839	0.1502	0.1228	0.0826	0.0560	0.0382	0.0262	0.0181	0.0074
23	0.7954	0.6342	0.5067	0.4057	0.3256	0.2618	0.2109	0.1703	0.1378	0.1117	0.0738	0.0491	0.0329	0.0222	0.0151	0.0059
24	0.7876	0.6217	0.4919	0.3901	0.3101	0.2470	0.1971	0.1577	0.1264	0.1015	0.0659	0.0431	0.0284	0.0188	0.0126	0.0047

Present Value of an Annuity

PRESENT VALUE OF AN ANNUITY

Period, n	Discount Rate, k																			
	1%	2%	3%	4%	5%	6%	7%	8%	9%	10%	11%	12%	13%	14%	15%	16%	17%	18%	19%	20%
1	0.990	0.980	0.971	0.962	0.952	0.943	0.935	0.926	0.917	0.909	0.901	0.893	0.885	0.877	0.870	0.862	0.855	0.847	0.840	0.833
2	1.970	1.942	1.913	1.886	1.859	1.833	1.808	1.783	1.759	1.736	1.713	1.690	1.668	1.647	1.626	1.605	1.585	1.566	1.547	1.528
3	2.941	2.884	2.829	2.775	2.723	2.673	2.624	2.577	2.531	2.487	2.444	2.402	2.361	2.322	2.283	2.246	2.210	2.174	2.140	2.106
4	3.902	3.808	3.717	3.630	3.546	3.465	3.387	3.312	3.240	3.170	3.102	3.037	2.974	2.914	2.855	2.798	2.743	2.690	2.639	2.589
5	4.853	4.713	4.580	4.452	4.329	4.212	4.100	3.993	3.890	3.791	3.696	3.605	3.517	3.433	3.352	3.274	3.199	3.127	3.058	2.991
6	5.795	5.601	5.417	5.242	5.076	4.917	4.767	4.623	4.486	4.355	4.231	4.111	3.998	3.889	3.784	3.685	3.589	3.498	3.410	3.326
7	6.728	6.472	6.230	6.002	5.786	5.582	5.389	5.206	5.033	4.868	4.712	4.564	4.423	4.288	4.160	4.039	3.922	3.812	3.706	3.605
8	7.652	7.325	7.020	6.733	6.463	6.210	5.971	5.747	5.535	5.335	5.146	4.968	4.799	4.639	4.487	4.344	4.207	4.078	3.954	3.837
9	8.566	8.162	7.786	7.435	7.108	6.802	6.515	6.247	5.995	5.759	5.537	5.328	5.132	4.946	4.772	4.607	4.451	4.303	4.163	4.031
10	9.471	8.983	8.530	8.111	7.722	7.360	7.024	6.710	6.418	6.145	5.889	5.650	5.426	5.216	5.019	4.833	4.659	4.494	4.339	4.192
11	10.368	9.787	9.253	8.760	8.306	7.887	7.499	7.139	6.805	6.495	6.207	5.938	5.687	5.453	5.234	5.029	4.836	4.656	4.486	4.327
12	11.255	10.575	9.954	9.385	8.863	8.384	7.943	7.536	7.161	6.814	6.492	6.194	5.918	5.660	5.421	5.197	4.988	4.793	4.611	4.439
13	12.134	11.348	10.635	9.986	9.394	8.853	8.358	7.904	7.487	7.103	6.750	6.424	6.122	5.842	5.583	5.342	5.118	4.910	4.715	4.533
14	13.004	12.106	11.296	10.563	9.899	9.295	8.745	8.244	7.786	7.367	6.982	6.628	6.302	6.002	5.724	5.468	5.229	5.008	4.802	4.611
15	13.865	12.849	11.938	11.118	10.380	9.712	9.108	8.559	8.061	7.606	7.191	6.811	6.462	6.142	5.847	5.575	5.324	5.092	4.876	4.675
16	14.718	13.578	12.561	11.652	10.838	10.106	9.447	8.851	8.313	7.824	7.379	6.974	6.604	6.265	5.954	5.668	5.405	5.162	4.938	4.730
17	15.562	14.292	13.166	12.166	11.274	10.477	9.763	9.122	8.544	8.022	7.549	7.120	6.729	6.373	6.047	5.749	5.475	5.222	4.990	4.775
18	16.398	14.992	13.754	12.659	11.690	10.828	10.059	9.372	8.756	8.201	7.702	7.250	6.840	6.467	6.128	5.818	5.534	5.273	5.033	4.812
19	17.226	15.678	14.324	13.134	12.085	11.158	10.336	9.604	8.950	8.365	7.839	7.366	6.938	6.550	6.198	5.877	5.584	5.316	5.070	4.843
20	18.046	16.351	14.877	13.590	12.462	11.470	10.594	9.818	9.129	8.514	7.963	7.469	7.025	6.623	6.259	5.929	5.628	5.353	5.101	4.870
21	18.857	17.011	15.415	14.029	12.821	11.764	10.836	10.017	9.292	8.649	8.075	7.562	7.102	6.687	6.312	5.973	5.665	5.384	5.127	4.891
22	19.660	17.658	15.937	14.451	13.163	12.042	11.061	10.201	9.442	8.772	8.176	7.645	7.170	6.743	6.359	6.011	5.696	5.410	5.149	4.909
23	20.456	18.292	16.444	14.857	13.489	12.303	11.272	10.371	9.580	8.883	8.266	7.718	7.230	6.792	6.399	6.044	5.723	5.432	5.167	4.925
24	21.243	18.914	16.936	15.247	13.799	12.550	11.469	10.529	9.707	8.985	8.348	7.784	7.283	6.835	6.434	6.073	5.746	5.451	5.182	4.937
25	22.023	19.523	17.413	15.622	14.094	12.783	11.654	10.675	9.823	9.077	8.422	7.843	7.330	6.873	6.464	6.097	5.766	5.467	5.195	4.948
26	22.795	20.121	17.877	15.983	14.375	13.003	11.826	10.810	9.929	9.161	8.488	7.896	7.372	6.906	6.491	6.118	5.783	5.480	5.206	4.956
27	23.560	20.707	18.327	16.330	14.643	13.211	11.987	10.935	10.027	9.237	8.548	7.943	7.409	6.935	6.514	6.136	5.798	5.492	5.215	4.964
28	24.316	21.281	18.764	16.663	14.898	13.406	12.137	11.051	10.116	9.307	8.602	7.984	7.441	6.961	6.534	6.152	5.810	5.502	5.223	4.970
29	25.066	21.844	19.188	16.984	15.141	13.591	12.278	11.158	10.198	9.370	8.650	8.022	7.470	6.983	6.551	6.166	5.820	5.510	5.229	4.975
30	25.808	22.396	19.600	17.292	15.372	13.765	12.409	11.258	10.274	9.427	8.694	8.055	7.496	7.003	6.566	6.177	5.829	5.517	5.235	4.979
35	29.409	24.999	21.487	18.665	16.374	14.498	12.948	11.655	10.567	9.644	8.855	8.176	7.586	7.070	6.617	6.215	5.858	5.539	5.251	4.992
40	32.835	27.355	23.115	19.793	17.159	15.046	13.332	11.925	10.757	9.779	8.951	8.244	7.634	7.105	6.642	6.233	5.871	5.548	5.258	4.997
45	36.095	29.490	24.519	20.720	17.774	15.456	13.606	12.108	10.881	9.863	9.008	8.283	7.661	7.123	6.654	6.242	5.877	5.552	5.261	4.999
50	39.196	31.424	25.730	21.482	18.256	15.762	13.801	12.233	10.962	9.915	9.042	8.304	7.675	7.133	6.661	6.246	5.880	5.554	5.262	4.999

Future Value of an Annuity

Period, n	Compound Rate, k																			
	1%	2%	3%	4%	5%	6%	7%	8%	9%	10%	11%	12%	13%	14%	15%	16%	17%	18%	19%	20%
1	1.000	1.000	1.000	1.000	1.000	1.000	1.000	1.000	1.000	1.000	1.000	1.000	1.000	1.000	1.000	1.000	1.000	1.000	1.000	1.000
2	2.010	2.020	2.030	2.040	2.050	2.060	2.070	2.080	2.090	2.100	2.110	2.120	2.130	2.140	2.150	2.160	2.170	2.180	2.190	2.200
3	3.030	3.060	3.091	3.122	3.152	3.184	3.215	3.246	3.278	3.310	3.342	3.374	3.407	3.440	3.473	3.506	3.539	3.572	3.606	3.640
4	4.060	4.122	4.184	4.246	4.310	4.375	4.440	4.506	4.573	4.641	4.710	4.779	4.850	4.921	4.993	5.066	5.141	5.215	5.291	5.368
5	5.101	5.204	5.309	5.416	5.526	5.637	5.751	5.867	5.985	6.105	6.228	6.353	6.480	6.610	6.742	6.877	7.0:4	7.154	7.297	7.442
6	6.152	6.308	6.468	6.633	6.802	6.975	7.153	7.336	7.523	7.716	7.913	8.115	8.323	8.536	8.754	8.977	9.207	9.442	9.683	9.930
7	7.214	7.434	7.662	7.898	8.142	8.394	8.654	8.923	9.200	9.487	9.783	10.089	10.405	10.730	11.067	11.414	11.772	12.142	12.523	12.916
8	8.286	8.583	8.892	9.214	9.549	9.897	10.260	10.637	11.028	11.436	11.859	12.300	12.757	13.233	13.727	14.240	14.773	15.327	15.902	16.499
9	9.369	9.755	10.159	10.583	11.027	11.491	11.978	12.488	13.021	13.579	14.164	14.776	15.416	16.085	16.786	17.519	18.285	19.086	19.923	20.799
10	10.462	10.950	11.464	12.006	12.578	13.181	13.816	14.487	15.193	15.937	16.722	17.549	18.420	19.337	20.304	21.321	22.393	23.521	24.709	25.959
11	11.567	12.169	12.808	13.486	14.207	14.972	15.784	16.645	17.560	18.531	19.561	20.655	21.814	23.045	24.349	25.733	27.200	28.755	30.404	32.150
12	12.683	13.412	14.192	15.026	15.917	16.870	17.888	18.977	20.141	21.384	22.713	24.133	25.650	27.271	29.002	30.850	32.824	34.931	37.180	39.581
13	13.809	14.680	15.618	16.627	17.713	18.882	20.141	21.495	22.953	24.523	26.212	28.029	29.985	32.089	34.352	36.786	39.404	42.219	45.244	48.497
14	14.947	15.974	17.086	18.292	19.599	21.015	22.550	24.215	26.019	27.975	30.095	32.393	34.883	37.581	40.505	43.672	47.103	50.818	54.841	59.196
15	16.097	17.293	18.599	20.024	21.579	23.276	25.129	27.152	29.361	31.772	34.405	37.280	40.417	43.842	47.580	51.660	56.110	60.965	66.261	72.035
16	17.258	18.639	20.157	21.825	23.657	25.673	27.888	30.324	33.003	35.950	39.190	42.753	46.672	50.980	55.717	60.925	66.649	72.939	79.850	87.442
17	18.430	20.012	21.762	23.698	25.840	28.213	30.840	33.750	36.974	40.545	44.501	48.884	53.739	59.118	65.075	71.673	78.979	87.068	96.022	105.93
18	19.615	21.412	23.414	25.645	28.132	30.906	33.999	37.450	41.301	45.599	50.396	55.750	61.725	68.394	75.836	84.141	93.406	103.74	115.27	128.12
19	20.811	22.841	25.117	27.671	30.539	33.760	37.379	41.446	46.018	51.159	56.939	63.440	70.749	78.969	88.212	98.603	110.28	123.41	138.17	154.74
20	22.019	24.297	26.870	29.778	33.066	36.786	40.996	45.762	51.160	57.275	64.203	72.052	80.947	91.025	102.44	115.38	130.03	146.63	165.42	186.69
21	23.239	25.783	28.676	31.969	35.719	39.993	44.865	50.423	56.765	64.002	72.265	81.699	92.470	104.77	118.81	134.84	153.14	174.02	197.85	225.03
22	24.472	27.299	30.537	34.248	38.505	43.392	49.006	55.457	62.873	71.403	81.214	92.503	105.49	120.44	137.63	157.41	180.17	206.34	236.44	271.03
23	25.716	28.845	32.453	36.618	41.430	46.996	53.436	60.893	69.532	79.543	91.148	104.60	120.20	138.30	159.28	183.60	211.80	244.49	282.36	326.24
24	26.973	30.422	34.426	39.083	44.502	50.816	58.177	66.765	76.790	88.497	102.17	118.16	136.83	158.66	184.17	213.98	248.81	289.49	337.01	392.48
25	28.243	32.030	36.459	41.646	47.727	54.865	63.249	73.106	84.701	98.347	114.41	133.33	155.62	181.87	212.79	249.21	292.10	342.60	402.04	471.98
26	29.526	33.671	38.553	44.312	51.113	59.156	68.676	79.954	93.324	109.18	128.00	150.33	176.85	208.33	245.71	290.09	342.76	405.27	479.43	567.38
27	30.821	35.344	40.710	47.084	54.669	63.706	74.484	87.351	102.72	121.10	143.08	169.37	200.84	238.50	283.57	337.50	402.03	479.22	571.52	681.85
28	32.129	37.051	42.931	49.968	58.403	68.528	80.698	95.339	112.97	134.21	159.82	190.70	227.95	272.89	327.10	392.50	471.38	566.48	681.11	819.22
29	33.450	38.792	45.219	52.966	62.323	73.640	87.347	103.97	124.14	148.63	178.40	214.58	258.58	312.09	377.17	456.30	552.51	669.45	811.52	984.07
30	34.785	40.568	47.575	56.085	66.439	79.058	94.461	113.28	136.31	164.49	199.02	241.33	293.20	356.79	434.75	530.31	647.44	790.95	966.71	1181.9
35	41.660	49.994	60.462	73.652	90.320	111.43	138.24	172.32	215.71	271.02	341.59	431.66	546.68	693.57	881.17	1120.7	1426.5	1816.7	2314.2	2948.3
40	48.886	60.402	75.401	95.026	120.80	154.76	199.64	259.06	337.88	442.59	581.83	767.09	1013.7	1342.0	1779.1	2360.8	3134.5	4163.2	5529.8	7343.9
45	56.481	71.893	92.720	121.03	159.70	212.74	285.75	386.51	525.86	718.90	986.64	1358.2	1874.2	2590.6	3585.1	4965.3	6879.3	9531.6	13203	18281
50	64.463	84.579	112.80	152.67	209.35	290.34	406.53	573.77	815.08	1163.9	1668.8	2400.0	3459.5	4994.5	7217.7	10435	15089	21813	31515	45497

Resources for the Growing Business

Online Resources

www.numbers101.com

Our official website is packed full of articles, advice, and business tools such as cashflow spreadsheets, templates and links. You can also sign up for our free newsletter and join our online Numbers 101 community, linking small businesses all over the world!

www.self-counsel.com

Online shopping for a wide variety of business and legal titles (including this one and other titles in the *Numbers 101 for Small Business* series).

www.sba.gov

US Small Business Administration — lots of great resources for small businesses. Mostly US focused but useful for companies in all countries.

www.cfib.ca

Canadian Federation of Independent Business. CFIB is an advocacy group for small businesses. They lobby the government for legislative changes that will assist businesses and their owners. On the website are lease-versus-buy calculators, downloadable publications, and other resources.

http://sme.ic.gc.ca

Performance Plus from Industry Canada. A great website for businesses from all countries. Shows you how your business stacks up with others in your industry.

www.bcentral.com

Microsoft Small Business Resources. Do they want to sell you stuff? Of course! In addition, this website also offers great articles on marketing, promotion, and other business matters.

www.toolkit.cch.com

CCH Business Owner's Toolkit. Great tools and resources, including sample business documents, checklists, and government forms.

www.inc.com

The online presence of *Inc.* magazine. Here you will find great articles, tools, and calculators to help your business grow.

Must-Read Books for Entrepreneurs

Building a Shared Vision: A Leader's Guide to Aligning the Organization by C. Patrick Lewis (Oregon: Productivity Press, 1997)

This book helps you to bring your vision down to the organization level.

Good to Great: Why Some Companies Make the Leap and Others Don't by Jim Collins (New York: Harper Business, 2001)

Whether you have one employee or thousands, this book will show you how great leaders make great companies.

Inside the Magic Kingdom: Seven Keys to Disney's Success by Tom Connellan (Bard Press, 1997).

A look at one of the most successful team-oriented companies in the world.

From Worst to First: Behind the Scenes of Continental's Remarkable Comeback by Gordon Bethune (Wiley, 1999).

This book follows Continental's meteoric rise in three years from its mediocre beginnings. A great case study on how strong leadership can make fantastic changes in an organization.

Pour Your Heart Into It: How Starbucks Built a Company One Cup at a Time by Howard Schultz (Hyperion, 1999).

Starbucks began with the vision of its CEO and the author of this book, Howard Schultz. He has turned it into a marketing phenomenon and one of the fastest growing companies in the world.

Body and Soul by Anita Roddick (Crown Publishing, 1991).

When Roddick started The Body Shop, she had a very different vision in mind than most entrepreneurs. She showed us that it is possible to succeed by marching to the beat of your own drummer!

The Nordstrom Way: The Inside Story of America's #1 Customer Service Company by Robert Spector & Patrick D. McCarthy (Wiley, 1996).

Customer service can make or break a company. Learn how Nordstrom has made rabidly loyal customers and how you can too.

McDonald's: Behind the Arches by John F. Love (Bantam, 1995).

An inside look at the most successful franchise on the planet.

Virgin King: Inside Richard Branson's Business Empire by Tim Jackson (HarperCollins, 1998).

Richard Branson is one of the most individual and successful entrepreneurs in the world. Learn how he took Virgin Airlines from its humble beginnings to become one of the most-loved and profitable underdogs.

Nuts! Southwest Airlines' Crazy Recipe for Business and Personal Success by Kevin Freiberg and Jackie Freiberg (Broadway Books, 1998).

There is no other business model quite like Southwest Airlines'. They have truly listened to their customers and have developed fantastic systems to help them meet their goals. A great book on systemization and an in-depth look at a fascinating company.

Glossary

Annuity: A series of constant or level cash flows that occurs at the end of each period for a fixed number of periods.

Balance sheet: One of the three major financial statements of a business. (The statement of cash flow and the income statement are the other two.) The balance sheet displays everything of a measurable financial value that is owned and owed by the company.

Budgeting: The process of planning and projecting revenues, expenses, and capital expenditures for future fiscal periods.

Business risk: The total amount of danger of loss a business faces from both internal and external factors, such as competition, foreign exchange rate changes, inadequate internal management, and market concentration.

Capacity: The upper limit of a business's ability to produce a product or service.

Capital: The resources that a business uses to produce a product or service.

Cash flow: The inflows to and outflows from a business, regardless of the source.

Cash flow statement (also known as the statement of changes in financial position or the statement of cash flows): One of the three major financial statements of a business. (The balance sheet and income statement are the other two.) The cash flow statement, in its most general terms, shows why there is an increase or decrease in cash during the year.

Controller (comptroller): The "big cheese" accountant in an organization. The controller oversees all accounting functions and sometimes operates as the company's chief financial officer.

Conversion rate: The number of potential customers who buy versus the number who inquire about your product or service.

Corporation: One of the three major forms of business ownership (partnership and sole proprietorship are the other two). A corporation is the only type of business that is legally separate from its owners: it is itself a legal entity. Corporate ownership is shown through the issues of share certificates.

Creditor: A person or other business that has loaned money or extended credit to a business.

Debt: The amounts owed by a business to outside persons or businesses. It is sometimes more narrowly defined as to exclude accounts payable and include only loans that have fixed interest rates and repayment schedules.

Debt financing: The amount of capital raised by a business through borrowing. Sources of debt financing include banks, trust companies, credit cards, and leasing companies.

Decline: The last of three stages in a company's life cycle, in which revenues and customer base begin to decline. The other two are infancy and maturity.

Demand: The desire by consumers for a business's product.

Dividends: The portion of earnings (either current or retained from prior periods) that have been distributed out to the shareholders in the current operating period.

Dun & Bradstreet: A corporate rating agency in the United States.

Earnings: A term usually used interchangeably with net income (i.e., revenues less expenses).

Entrepreneur: A person who envisions and creates a business. This person may or may not be either an investor or manager in the ongoing operations.

Equity: The total amount of recoverable capital the owners of a business have invested.

Equity financing: The amount of capital raised through the sale of partial ownership in a business.

Exit strategy: A plan for a business's owners to either sell or wind up the business.

Franchise: A company that designs and builds a business model for entrepreneurs to follow.

General ledger: The grouping of accounts used by a business. Also, the book where the main summary records are kept for each balance sheet and income statement item.

General journal: A detailed record of all financial transactions of a business. The general journal is summarized and entered as net increases and decreases to the accounts in the general ledger.

Goodwill: The value of a business that is not directly attributable to hard assets but instead to the benefits such as a business's reputation or customer list.

Gross income: Another term for revenues.

Gross margin: Represents revenues minus the cost of goods sold in the period.

Hard systems: Those business systems that involve tangible procedures, for example, how a management report is prepared.

Income statement: One of the three major financial statements of a business. (The balance sheet and statement of cash flow are the other two.) The income statement shows operating activity over an operating period from revenues, expenses, and extraordinary gains and losses.

Infancy: The first of three stages in a company's life cycle, in which revenues increase exponentially and cash flow is generally strained. The other two are maturity and decline.

Insolvent: A term used to describe a business that does not have enough assets to meet its debt obligations in the short term. Insolvency can lead to bankruptcy if not corrected quickly.

Internal control: Represents the procedures set up in a business to prevent errors and fraudulent activity.

Inventory: Goods held for resale that remain unsold at the end of an operating period. In a manufacturing environment, inventory includes raw materials, goods in the process of being made, and finished goods. In certain service industries, inventory includes time spent on customer activities but not yet billed out.

Life cycle of a business: Represents the three stages of the total existence of a business (infancy, maturity, and decline).

Management operational plan: A company's plan for how it will do business on a day-to-day basis. A management operational plan will include short-term budgets and revenue forecasts as well as analysis of historical performance (see the second book in the Numbers 101 for Small Business series, *Financial Management 101*, for a more complete discussion of the management operational plan).

Manager: The individual that oversees the production staff and ensures that policies and procedures are being followed.

Market niche: The specific set of consumer demands that are met by a business.

Market share: The number of customers a business has as compared to all of the customers for that particular product or service.

Maturity: The second of three stages in a company's life cycle, in which revenues and customer base are steady and customer demand has been sated. The other two are infancy and decline.

Mission statement: A company's representation of its vision and how it will achieve it.

Net income: The income left in an accounting period after all expenses have been deducted from revenues. The term net income is used only if the revenues exceed the expenses.

Net loss: The deficit for an accounting period that occurs when the expenses for that period exceed the revenues.

Partnership: One of the three major forms of business ownership. (corporation and sole proprietor are the other two.) A partnership is an unincorporated business with two or more owners. Partnerships are jointly owned by the partners and do not have a separate "legal life" of their own.

Profit: see Net income.

Profit and loss (P&L) statement: Another name for an income statement.

Return on investment (ROI): The amount of investment income an investor makes on an investment divided by the amount invested.

Revenue: The amount of net assets generated by a business as a

result of its operations.

Script: A written and rehearsed dialogue for staff members to use when dealing with customers or potential customers to ensure the consistency of the message.

Shareholder: An owner or internal investor of a corporation.

Soft systems: Those business systems that involve intangible procedures, more particularly, the actions of employees. For

example, how a customer is greeted on the telephone or how a customer complaint is handled.

Sole proprietorship: One of the three major forms of business ownership. (Corporation and partnership are the other two.) A sole proprietorship is an unincorporated company owned by a single owner. It has no "legal life" of its own.

Solvency: The ability of a company to settle its liabilities with its assets.

Statement of cash flows: One of the three major financial statements. The statement of cash flow explains the changes in assets, liabilities, and net equity for the period.

Statement of changes in financial position: An older term for the statement of cash flows.

Stockholder: see Shareholder.

Systems: The group of business systems that make up the operations of a company.

Turnkey: A business that has had policies and procedures well-documented and tested so that anyone can run it successfully from the very beginning.

Vision statement: A company's overall statement as to how it views itself in the future. A vision statement is broken down further into a measurable mission statement and actionable operational goals.